A Philosophy
of
Universality

Translated from the French
Original title : UNE PHILOSOPHIE DE L'UNIVERSEL

Omraam Mikhaël Aïvanhov

A Philosophy
of
Universality

3rd edition

Collection Izvor
No. 206

EDITIONS PROSVETA

Editions Prosveta S.A. – B.P. 12 – 83601 Fréjus Cedex (France)

ISBN 2-85566-420-9

édition originale : ISBN 2-85566-187-0

TABLE OF CONTENTS

The reader will better understand certain aspects of the lectures published in the present volume if he bears in mind that the Master Omraam Mikhaël Aïvanhov's Teaching is exclusively oral.

I

WHAT IS A SECT ?

For thousands of years, human beings have been in the habit of paying attention to the form, the external wrappings that are visible to the eye, and of neglecting the inner content and the hidden meaning of things. And the Sacred Scriptures also have form, content and meaning : they are no exception to the general rule. The form — the story — is for the man in the street ; the moral, symbolic content is for the disciple who strives to grasp its underlying message and put it into practice, and the hidden spiritual meaning is for the Initiate who is capable of interpreting it.

The great Initiates have always been builders of new forms. They have always recognized the need for forms, but those they introduced were alive, imbued with a science that the average human being was incapable of deciphering, precisely because of this ingrained habit of heeding only what can be seen, touched or heard. Of course, it is true that forms can be helpful and stimulating, but they would be far more so if men could feel and understand the truths they contained and put them into practice in their lives. Every religion has a body of esoteric teachings that exists alongside its exoteric doctrines, for there has always been an elite who felt the need for a deeper understanding of the mysteries of creation. The meagre scraps that satisfied the masses were never enough for them. In the Christian Church, alongside the mainstream Church of St. Peter, to which the great majority of believers belonged, another stream has always existed and flourished in secret : the Church of St. John, guardian of the true spirituality, the true philosophy of Christ.

This question of spirit and form is very far-reaching. You have only to observe human beings to see that most of them are so obsessed by form that they end by identifying with it. In this way they actually identify with their own physical body. Whatever they do, they do for the benefit of their physical body ; they cannot see their spirit, so they don't bother with it ! They do not realize that in this way they are only weakening themselves, and that they will become more and more like animals, for true strength and light have not been given to the physical body. If they identify with the physical body (the form), they will never develop their spirit which is eternal, immortal and omniscient, a spark of God Himself.

The materialistic philosophy so prevalent today severely restricts the scope of men's lives, for when they are no longer enlightened, guided and inspired by the spirit, they shrivel up and become small-minded and sectarian. They judge everything in life from their own, strictly limited point of view, in the firm belief that it is the best. And how wrong they are ! A materialistic point of view is hopelessly biased and sectarian. Yes, sectarianism exists in every area : economics, politics, science, religion, philosophy, the arts... everywhere. And I shall prove it to you.

The notion of sector is a common one today. In the language of geometry, a sector is a wedge-shaped 'slice' of a circle ; in a city or a country, the word sector is used to indicate a specific region, and in the human body which forms a perfect whole, an organ could be termed a sector. But then, what is a sect ? Well, it is quite simple : once a religion has achieved official status, it declares that any group that refuses its dogmas, beliefs or practices is a sect. It is the official Church that pronounces this judgment, and history tells of countless thousands who have been thrown into prison, persecuted or burnt at the stake because they refused to adhere to the doctrines of a Church ! Later, history pronounces its own judgment on the judgments of that Church !

But now let me tell you something that you do not know — something that is quite new to you. It is this : it is not up to human beings to decide who is sectarian and who is not : that decision belongs to Nature alone. Take the case of a member of a Church who works for the propagation of the faith : his fellow believers would never think of accusing him of sectarianism, would they ? No, but perhaps Nature has another point of view, other criteria by which she judges him ; she may well condemn him for his sectarianism ! Yes, Nature may condemn him for being sectarian and sentence him to bed, to hospital — or even to the grave ! Why ? Because his way of thinking and behaving contradicts certain laws of living, intelligent Nature. He neglects these laws ; perhaps he has never even known that they existed ; his life is not in harmony with the Whole, and, in spite of the opinion of the faithful of his Church, he has to be classed as a sectarian. Whereas Nature may show her approval of someone who has been condemned as sectarian by those same faithful, by showering him with health, peace and perfect fulfilment. Why allow those who have no discernment to judge ? Cosmic Intelligence alone is in a position to know if we are sectarian or not.

If you observe what goes on in the world, you see that each individual chooses his activities according to his temperament and tastes, or according to external conditions and circumstances, without taking into account his need to develop and grow on every level of his being. Man is endowed with a mind, a heart and a will, and he must develop and function in all three dimensions if he is to manifest himself as a fully balanced human being. Experience shows that those who are equally developed in the three areas of thought, feelings and actions are very rare. You will find many intellectuals who are heartless and lacking in will-power ; others have a strong will but are utterly brainless and so on. Yes, we see nothing but cripples all round us : people who are gifted in one area and handicapped to a greater or lesser degree in all the others.

And yet, if we question Cosmic Intelligence about it, It will tell us that man was created in order to be in the image of his Creator, capable of understanding and loving perfection and of achieving it here, on earth. Why did Jesus say, 'Be perfect just as your Father in heaven is perfect' ? Because he knew all this ! He knew that man had been created to become omniscient, all-powerful and all-loving just like his Heavenly Father. And this is why all those who have only developed the things that came most easily to them, whether it be mathematics, poetry, music, swimming or anything else (yes, if you look at them, you will see that most of them do nothing but cultivate one very limited area), are sectarians. And what is so serious is that they don't know it !

Man must grow and develop on the three levels of mind, heart and will. He must understand, love and accomplish. But what must he accomplish ? He must accomplish the Kingdom of God and His Righteousness on earth ; this is the only way to be 'saved'. Man will not be saved by the means that most Christians believe in. Do you really think that faith and a few good works are sufficient to win you a place in Heaven at the right hand of God ? Poor Lord, what He is going to have to put up with, surrounded by coarse, ignorant men, by gluttons, drunkards, smokers and dissipated libertines ! It doesn't matter what kind of lives they led, they had faith and considered themselves to be upright men, so they will go straight to Heaven when they die ? Don't you believe it ! Let me tell you what is going to happen to them.

There was once an Orthodox priest in Bulgaria who never stopped scolding his wife. He kept telling her she was an ignorant sinner, whereas he was a model of perfection. One day he felt that his last hours had come, so he bade farewell to his wife, saying, 'Goodbye, my dear. I shall be waiting for you in Heaven.' Not long after, the wife died and went to Heaven, and there she started to look for her darling husband, but he was nowhere to be found ! Finally, she went and asked St. Peter, who looked through his big register but couldn't find the priest's name anywhere. 'I can't find him' said

St. Peter ; 'He must be in the basement !' And he
gave her a pass to go and look for him in Hell. When
she got down there, there was her husband, up to
his neck in a cauldron of boiling water. 'Oh, my
poor husband !' exclaimed the good woman ;
'What a terrible fix you're in !' 'Don't be too sorry
for me' replied her husband ; 'I'm relatively well
off. I'm standing on the Archbishop's shoulders !'

And that is what happens to many of those who
think that they are just and upright men : they go
and spend a little while in Hell before coming back
to earth to learn to develop themselves and reach
perfection. In the eyes of universal Initiatic Science,
almost all human beings are sectarian as long as they
are still not perfect.

And what about the tendency that we see all
round us, to work for the aggrandizement of one
group, whether it be a Union, a political party or
a country ? Of course it is considered to be so
generous, but in fact it is still too personal and
egocentric. Just as long as your activity does not
aim at the goal of peace and happiness for the whole
of mankind, it is limited and, therefore, sectarian.
Since even science tells us that we are part of cosmic
life ; since we owe our very existence not only to
the earth, the water, the air and the sun, but also
to the stars, why must we always huddle up in a corner with our own petty interests ?

And while we are on the subject : have you ever discovered the secrets of that earth, water, air and fire to which we owe our existence ? You will ask : 'What secrets ? What is there to understand ?' A great many things, and one of them is this : look at the planet Earth, the surface occupied by dry land is relatively little, the surface covered by water is a great deal more, the amount of space filled with air is far greater again, and that filled by fire and light stretches infinite distances into space. And this means that we, too, should try to stretch out to infinity.

Then, too, consider this : how long can you survive if you are deprived of these elements ? You can survive without solid food for fifty or sixty days ; without liquids for only about ten days ; without air for only a few minutes, and without heat ? At the very instant your heart loses its heat you die ! And this shows that the solid element is less important than the liquid, that the liquid is less important than the gaseous, and that the gaseous element is less important again than the etheric, igneous element : heat and light.

So you see, what man needs most is that etheric element that fills the whole of space. And this being so, why do human beings cling to the petty little things of everyday life so fiercely that they allow themselves to be overwhelmed and ground down by them, instead of seeking the freedom of immensity and universality ? The answer is this : because they have a sectarian mentality. Look at all those who are dedicated to religion, politics or economics : you will find that they are all sectarian ! But as they will be the last to see the truth, they all agree on one thing : that war must be waged against sects !

It may be perfectly true, of course, that there are some sects that are doing a lot of harm (but I could not tell you which ones, because that is not my business ; my work lies elsewhere), so it is only normal to want to limit the amount of damage they can do. But those who decide what measures to take must themselves be absolutely honest and free from prejudice, and capable of determining which groups are creating anarchy and disorder and which ones are working to bring peace, justice and happiness to all men ; which ones, in other words, are working for the Kingdom of God and the coming of the Golden Age.

And now, let me tell you something which constitutes a synthesis, a summary of the whole of Initiatic philosophy. There is a woman in Bulgaria called Vanga, who is one of the world's greatest clairvoyants. She has often given such irrefutable proof of her psychic powers, that even the government consults her, and there is a hotel near her home, built by the State, to accommodate the visitors who come from all over the world. A particularly striking thing about Vanga is that she is blind ; those who want to consult her give her a lump of sugar that they have handled and, thanks to this lump of sugar, she can tell them everything, with the most astounding accuracy, about their past, present and future.

How is this possible ? It is perfectly simple ! Every single being emanates quantities of minute, invisible, intangible particles, which are still unknown to science, and these particles settle on various objects and soak into them. This is how we all give something of our virtues, strengths and light — or, on the contrary, something of our illnesses, vices and impurities — to the people and things about us. Without knowing it, we do good, and without knowing it, we do evil. But even though we may not be aware of all this, our acts go down on record, and one day we shall be rewarded for the good and punished for the evil we have done.

So true religion is based on a science, a vast body of knowledge, that has grown out of the observation of phenomena which can only be perceived by certain highly evolved beings. Everyone is, of course, absolutely free to reject this science, but sooner or later they will see where that attitude of rejection leads them. In any event, let me tell you that anyone who knows nothing about this science is sectarian. Yes, if someone refuses to understand that his thoughts and feelings and inner states influence the whole collectivity, he is sectarian : he does what he pleases without a thought either for the ill effect his acts might have on others, or for the good he could do them. This attitude limits him and makes him sectarian.

2

NO CHURCH IS ETERNAL

Nations, countries and peoples, just like human beings, are born, grow up, get old and die, making way for others. They all follow the same pattern, giving the special gifts and treasures they have to give, and then fading away. It is as though they had to go away for a rest and, after a time, they will reappear and produce new treasures. History shows that this is the fate not only of nations but also of religions : a period of rapid growth leads to a profusion of spiritual fruits and widespread influence, but then it reaches a peak and, almost at once, begins to crystallize and lose the key to life. Even the Mysteries, even the great temples of ancient Egypt which once possessed the keys of knowledge and power... where are they today ? Where are all those hierophants ? What has become of all that science ? They have all had to submit to the unchanging laws of life.

Every form, that is to say, every object or living being born into this world, is obliged to die and make way for others. Only the spirit has no end, for it has no beginning ; and the spirit incarnates continually in new forms. God has not given the gift of eternity to form ; form is fragile and short-lived, it cannot withstand the assault of time. Only the principle, the spirit which belongs to the divine world, is indestructible and eternal.

This is something that human beings do not understand, and because they do not understand it they are forever trying to perpetuate forms. The tendency is particularly obvious in the case of religions which have clung to the same rites and doctrines for centuries ; they still do not realize that dogmas and rituals are forms, and that they cannot be made to endure. Life is a well-spring, a perpetual outpouring, and it is in constant need of new forms through which to express itself. So it is life itself that breaks up the old forms, for it is always seeking new instruments, new channels through which to reveal its new riches, new lights, new splendours. This is why, after a certain time, all forms must disappear so as to make way for new shades of expression and new, subtler manifestations.

A human being is the perfect illustration of this : when a person is young, his physical body is supple, pliant and alive, and it is thanks to the material qualities of his body that the spirit can express itself more and more perfectly through the medium of his mind, heart and will. Then, at some point he reaches the age at which his physical form begins to stiffen and crystallize, and the spirit, which cannot express itself through the medium of this shrunken, hardened form, is obliged to leave it before coming back in a new form.

It is important to observe what goes on in nature and draw the right conclusions in every domain. The Churches are making a great mistake by clinging obstinately to the forms they developed centuries ago. The form must constantly be improved and refined so that it may express always more fully and more perfectly the new currents that never cease to flow from Heaven. For Heaven has not ordained that everything must stay exactly the same for eternity.

You only have to look at all the new, unprecedented needs and tendencies springing up in human society : why should there not be new forms to match these new manifestations ? The Age of Aquarius is fast approaching, and it is going to overturn and shatter all the old forms and values that human beings thought of as permanent. Human beings see things their way, but Cosmic Intelligence has a very different point of view. The plans of Cosmic Intelligence are not those of human beings, and now, thanks to the new currents of Aquarius, It is going to turn the old order upside down so as to show human beings that they must not bury the spirit in old forms.

If something is to endure it must constantly renew itself. And if Christians are leaving the Church in such numbers, it is because it never renews itself. It continues to cling to old conceptions which are no longer valid today and which need to be replaced. Of course, I am not talking about the basic principles on which Christianity is built. There will never be anything more perfect than the principles given by Christ in the Gospels. But why does the Church still encumber itself with obsolete practices which no longer serve their purpose ?

A lot of people leave the Church because they think that science contradicts and nullifies the truths of the Gospels, but that only shows that they have not understood the first thing about it. On the contrary, let me tell you that the discoveries of science actually emphasize the truths of the Gospels.

I can show you — in fact, I have already done so — that not only does official science not contradict the truths taught by Initiatic Science, it even proves their veracity. But this is something that neither scientists nor religious people have yet understood. For me, there is no contradiction : science and religion go hand in hand ; in fact they both go hand in hand with art, too, for the three are intimately related. Science brings mankind light, religion brings warmth (love), and art brings creative activity. Why have we invented the gulf that now separates these three when Nature created them to work together in life ? Initiates have never separated them from each other, but now that Western culture has done so, religion no longer has a hold on scientists : they reject it out of hand. But they reject it, of course, because they do not possess *true* science. Their kind of science focuses exclusively on the physical, material world. They are ignorant of the one true science on which all the religions of the world have been founded : the science of the three worlds, material, psychic and spiritual. As for art, it wavers uncertainly between the two, rebelling first against one and then against the other.

In nature, I repeat, religion, science and art are one. If they are not one today it is because human beings have separated them, and as long as they continue to separate them, men will never find truth. Science, religion and art form a unified whole, thanks to which everything can be understood and explained. Science is a need of the intellect ; religion is a need of the heart, and art is a need of the will which seeks to express something, to create and build. And these three needs are closely related, for you begin by thinking something, but you have to feel it before you can make it a concrete reality.

As a matter of fact, I can tell you that many contemporary scientists are reincarnations of Initiates of the past, High Priests who had knowledge of the Mysteries. Those who discovered radio and television simply applied the knowledge they had acquired in the distant past. Yes, they were Initiates of ancient Egypt, for our era is connected in many ways to Egyptian civilization, and it is destined to see the revelation and application on the physical plane of the sacred science of ancient Egypt.

Christianity stands in need of some major transformations, for it is still living on old traditions which are not adapted to our day and age. Besides, if religion as we know it were really adequate, mankind would be much better off than it is. No, religion has been reduced to a series of empty forms. No wonder most people cannot take it seriously any longer ! More and more, they reflect and question what they are told, and the stock answers no longer satisfy them. In the past their faith was such that they were ready to swallow whatever the Church told them, because, for them, the Church was the authority : it was the Church that thought and made decisions for them. But today, nobody wants others to do their thinking for them. And this means that Christianity is going to have to accept new forms. And those new forms will also wear out, one day, and have to be replaced yet again.

The function of form is to keep the contents intact ; it is, as it were, a container, a protection, a limit. And this means that it is also a prison. And if the contents are not to remain eternally frozen within a form, that form must be opened and the contents poured into new, subtler, more flexible, more transparent forms. This is why nothing that exists on the physical plane is eternal.

Time has no effect on principles, but it does affect forms. To say that time destroys everything is only true in regard to forms. And Christians have not yet understood that the form in which their religion was given to them centuries ago cannot last for ever ; that they are going to have to change it. But no : they are very tenacious ; they don't want to change anything.

The Universal White Brotherhood brings no new principles with it, only new forms. That is to say, it proposes new methods so that the spirit may have greater possibilities to express and manifest itself. This is evolution : a change, a renewal of forms. Evolution has always been a subject of keen interest to naturalists ; some saying that it is form that evolves, and others saying that forms are predetermined from all eternity and that it is beings who move from one form to another. It is the second theory that is correct : forms do not evolve. All forms, whether of animals, insects or plants, pre-exist in the world of archetypes, and individual creatures assume these forms for a time and then abandon them and move on to others, exactly as actors put on a new mask for each new play.

So the spirit changes its form, but forms do not

evolve ; they were created from all eternity, and even those that are still unknown to us, the new forms of plants and animals, already exist as archetypes. And for us, too, new forms are ready and waiting, and as we advance in our evolution we shall assume these new forms, for we constantly have to abandon an old form and acquire a new, more flexible, purer, more luminous one. In this way, as we assume new forms, we shall acquire new and better means of action and manifestation, whereas if we remained prisoners of our old forms we would be limited, we could never make any progress. This is what Christians fail to understand : they cling to the idea that they must perpetuate the form. But it is just not possible ; it is in contradiction with the decrees of Cosmic Intelligence.

Form is already eternal ! Yes, but only in the workshops on high, in the world of archetypes. On that level all forms are eternal because they are there to serve Cosmic Intelligence. But if men try to perpetuate forms eternally on earth ; that is, if they cling obstinately to one particular form, they oblige the Invisible World to come and smash it to pieces in order to set them free. This may seem very cruel, but it is not a question of cruelty. It is a question of love ; the love of Heaven that obliges man to advance.

Besides, what happens to human beings from one incarnation to the next ? More often than not they change their sex. If you were a woman in a previous life, it was in order to learn to manifest the qualities of the feminine principle. And now that you are a man, you must learn to manifest other qualities.

This apparent cruelty on the part of the Invisible World which shatters old forms in order to create new ones, is not yet understood by the Church. But whether the Church understands or not, I guarantee that its old forms will be destroyed. However desperately Christians try to hang on to their old forms and prevent their destruction, the Invisible World is going to have to shatter them in order to set human beings free and allow them to evolve.

The Universal White Brotherhood is a new form of the religion of Christ. Oh, I know : Christians are going to exclaim in horror at that, and swear to oppose us, because they are convinced that they have to remain faithful to the traditions they inherited from the past. But they will not emerge victorious from this battle : the Invisible World will show them that they are mistaken. A new form is going to appear which will last for a certain time before it, too, makes way for yet another, more perfect form. As you see, I am being perfectly fair and honest with you ; I have no wish to mislead you by telling you that the form introduced by our

Teaching will be eternal. Once it has done its work it will make way for yet another new form which will be still more highly evolved and better adapted to the times.

When someone tells me that he cannot accept the Teaching of the Universal White Brotherhood because he is a Catholic, I tell him, 'Very well ; if you feel more at home in the Church, stay there ! But as for us, we are going to move on.' For, I ask you, what can you learn from all those sermons that explain nothing at all ? Who is to blame if people listen to them and then go on doing all the things they shouldn't ? They are leaving the Church because it does not have the answer to their questions and can do nothing to ease their anguish. The sermons they hear may be very poetic or highly moral... Oh, I entirely agree with what they say, but one cannot learn much from them, for they are not backed up by a science that is really capable of explaining the meaning and goal of human existence, the laws that govern it or how to behave in harmony with those laws. They are all words — just words — no mention of how to put any of it into practice ! But then, has Christendom ever actually put the Gospels into practice ? No, never ! You only have to see what goes on in the so-called Christian countries !

Anyone who has decided to work with the eternal, unchanging principles of Christ, belongs to the Universal White Brotherhood. He is not destroying anything ; he is not working against Christ ; he is not trying to promote a new religion. No, he is simply working to promote new forms. Whereas someone who clings to the old forms shows that he has not understood the principles. He relies on the form to save him, and when he goes to bed at night he sleeps soundly in the security of their protection. Yes, those who rely on the form have no trouble going to sleep ! If you want to evolve you would do better not to count on forms but to work with principles. Isn't this a far better, more beneficial ideal ? Christ Himself will come and tell you how magnificent it is, for it is written in the New Testament : 'For the letter kills but the spirit gives life.' And that is exactly what I am saying. Yes, I am constantly urging you to strengthen your bonds with the spirit that gives life.

All those who give priority to principles belong to the Universal White Brotherhood. Not to the Brotherhood here, on earth, but to that great Universal White Brotherhood which includes all the most luminous creatures in the universe. The role of the Brotherhood in the world is simply to provide those perfect, sublime beings with the means and possibilities for action, so that the Kingdom of God may be established on earth. It is in this sense that the Universal White Brotherhood can be seen as a new form of the religion of Christ. And he who works with the principles of Christ, therefore, belongs to the Universal White Brotherhood. It is quite possible that he may not even know of our existence, but that does not matter ; he is still a member of the Universal White Brotherhood.

It is laziness that makes people cling to forms. They have long since stopped working on the spiritual level so they take to strutting about decked in forms. Look at the Christians of today : they have no desire to learn or to understand, they oppose any kind of change, in the belief that they are being faithful to Christ, whereas, in reality, they are only being faithful to forms elaborated by human beings.

We must be faithful to God and not only to men. If you insist on being faithful to men, that is your own business ; I have nothing against it, but you will end up as dust. For what were they, all those people who ruled the Church for so many hundreds of years ? As often as not they were poor wretches, no different from all the others — when they were not actually criminals ! And if one of them manifested a higher degree of understanding he was immediately criticized and persecuted. Look at history and you will see for yourselves : all those who attempted to introduce reforms were rejected, excommunicated and burnt ! They should have known better and stuck to the existing forms ! But forms are not very productive ; all they can do is imprison human beings. Yes, forms are the perfect prison : if you are a prisoner of forms you can never escape.

God manifested Himself through Jesus. But before Jesus He had already manifested Himself through Moses. If Moses accomplished such great deeds it was because God was with him. And if Jesus came, it was because the Law of Moses had had its day, and the intransigence that characterized it was no longer suited to the plans that Cosmic Intelligence had devised for mankind. And if that were so then, why should Cosmic Intelligence not have other plans for today ?

Actually, in our day, even the forms of Initiation have changed. In ancient times, Initiation took place in the temples where the disciples had to go through ordeals by fire, air, water and earth. But nowadays, Initiation takes place in everyday life ; without their disciples being aware of it, Initiates place them in certain situations, confront them with certain problems and observe their reactions. All the ordeals of Initiation are in everyday life ; the four elements are in everyday life ; it is here that you have to show that you have conquered fear, greed, egoism, sensuality and so on. Yes, there are plenty of trials, especially for those who want to make progress on the path of Initiation : they must know in advance that their wishes will be fulfilled, but that, before they are, they will have to endure many trials and ordeals. When they are least expecting it, they will be put to the test in their daily lives, for all our ordeals take place in our everyday lives. Our slightest gesture is observed and weighed, and very often we fail the test because of some tiny detail, because we were keeping our energies for something more spectacular.

So you have to be wide awake and vigilant, and remember : every circumstance in life can be a test. On each occasion you will be judged on your performance by beings in the world above. If you pass your tests you will be given a diploma ; but unlike the diplomas given by our universities, which can be torn or burnt or defaced or stolen, the diploma that you receive from your examiners in the world above is printed on your face, on your whole being, and no one can ever take it from you. And the spirits of nature, who know how to read that kind of diploma, will show you their appreciation by bidding you welcome and helping you. Wherever you go, throughout space, they will see your diploma. But if you fail your exams and receive no diploma, they will have no consideration or esteem for you ; they may even persecute you, because they will judge you to be a weak, ignorant, useless being.

So always remember this : everything that exists results from the relationship between the two opposite poles : spirit and matter, principles and forms. While they are on this earth, human beings are not capable of living with principles alone ; they need the support of forms. The spirit incarnates in the form of a body in order to manifest itself on the physical plane. When it returns to the regions of the spirit it does not need these forms, but while it is still on earth they are necessary. But it is important to know that forms do not last for long. God has not granted eternal life to forms ; this is why Heaven periodically sends Initiates or great Masters to change the existing forms — but only the forms, never the principles. I repeat : principles are unchangeable. Yes, for the principles are love, wisdom, truth and sacrifice, and these things will be valid for eternity.

3

THE SPIRIT BEHIND THE FORM

As long as you are on this earth you are obliged to live in the world of forms. And this means, for instance, that you have to retain and take care of the form of your body : it should be healthy, pleasant to look at and expressive ! For how long ? Until the time comes to move on to the other side.

In every area, including that of religion, a moment inevitably comes when one is obliged to discard a particular form, just as one discards a worn out garment. It must be kept only as long as it is indispensable or simply useful ; but as soon as it becomes obsolete it means that a new phase has begun, and we must either replace it or reach a much more profound understanding of it. For there are some rites, such as Baptism, Marriage, the Mass and Communion for instance, that are founded on eternal laws and the science of magic. This is particularly true of the Mass, which is pure white magic. In fact, it might be true to say that if the Church has endured until today, it is thanks to the Mass.

What a pity that a great many priests do not realize the profound significance of what they are doing when they celebrate Mass ! If they understood what they were doing, the power of the Mass would be even greater.

Most Christians have not yet understood the true religion brought by Christ. They go to church and light candles, bless themselves with Holy Water and receive Communion, but they have not understood that if these practices do not correspond to their inner frame of mind, they are hollow, meaningless gestures. They put up an icon of the Virgin Mary in their homes, and think that she will always be there to protect them, whatever they do. But that is nothing more than superstition : they believe in this and trust in that, but faith and belief are not the same thing. Most people think they have faith, but what they actually have is a set of beliefs. Yes, and this is because they are too attached to forms ; they don't realize that even prayers can be nothing but forms.

Once upon a time there was a monk who had the secret habit of paying frequent visits to the wine-cellar. It was his *péché mignon*, his favourite weakness ! And he was incapable of giving it up. Every evening he would say his prayers and ask God to forgive him, and then sleep soundly with a peaceful conscience. Yes, because, of course, all you have to do is to mutter a few prayers for forgiveness, and that puts everything right ! But one night he was rudely awakened from sleep by someone shaking him and saying : 'Wake up, wake up ! You forgot to say your prayers !' And who did he see beside his bed but the Devil himself ! And then he understood : if the Devil had taken the trouble to come and remind him to say his prayers, it was because it was to his advantage. If the monk continued to say his prayers in the belief that he was automatically forgiven, then he could go on drinking ! It was certainly not the Lord who had come to wake him up. The Lord does not hear a drunkard's prayers. So you see ? Often enough it is the Devil who hides behind forms and urges you to go to church, to light a candle, to say your prayers or go to Communion. In this way he helps you to become more and more deeply entrenched in these old forms, and never to make the slightest effort to work at improving yourself on a deeper level.

This is why, when I say that the Universal White Brotherhood is bringing a new religion, I am not claiming that it will be superior to the religion that Jesus brought. That is impossible ; Jesus truly reached the peak. There is nothing higher or more perfect than the law of love and sacrifice taught by Jesus. But on the level of methods, in the area of applications and interpretations, our Teaching has something new to offer, something that will help men to advance. The Gospels don't tell the whole

story ; there are still a great many obscure points
that need to be explained, and the Universal White
Brotherhood can provide those explanations, for it
is founded on authentic Initiatic Science.

Take the question of Baptism, for instance.
Catholics take a baby to church to be baptized when
it is only a few days old, and the priest anoints its
forehead with water and oil. He may very well be
thinking of other things while he is baptizing the
child, but that does not matter : thanks to the water
and oil, the stain of Original Sin is washed away
and the child becomes a member of the Christian
community and is saved once and for all ! The truth
is that the Church has greatly exaggerated the
efficacy of the rite of Baptism. It does not purify
someone for the rest of his life. How can anyone
believe that evil spirits will not dare to enter him
simply because a little water and Holy Oil was put
on his forehead when he was a baby ? No, unfortunately, the devils cannot be frightened away so
easily ; they are not at all impressed by Baptism.
It is up to each individual to work, all his life long,
to preserve and amplify the effects of Baptism, and
if he does not do so, it loses its efficacy.

You say that you have been baptized and the
stain of Original Sin has been washed away ! All
well and good, but you are going to have to work
during the rest of your life to preserve that purity.
Every day, with all your heart and soul, you must

consciously cleanse yourself. Some people feel so secure in the purifying effects of their baptism that they imagine that they need make no further effort to improve. But you only have to live with them to see that they are no better than those who have never been baptized — in fact they are a great deal worse ! This is why I say, 'You don't understand ! You must not let yourself be lulled into a false sense of security, thinking that you have been baptized and that Jesus has saved you. It is up to you to work at your own salvation.'

We read in the Old Testament, for example, of how the Prophet Elijah told the Syrian commander Naaman to wash himself seven times in the River Jordan in order to be cured of his leprosy. And Jesus, too, was baptized by John the Baptist in the Jordan. Baptism and ablutions are very potent rites, but their efficacy depends on the spiritual elevation of the person who baptizes you or tells you to wash yourself. And the same rule applies in the case of a talisman : the efficacy of a talisman depends on who prepares it : if he is weak and ignorant, the power of the talisman will also be weak. An object only becomes a talisman when it is impregnated with 'Telesma', 'that strength of all strengths' that Hermes Trismegistus speaks of in the Emerald Tablet. The efficacy of a talisman is entirely due to this power. If an object is not imbued with the power of Telesma it is not a talisman ; it is still just an object.

Water is an element that is particularly propitious to purification because of the invisible beings that dwell and work in it ; when a human being immerses himself in water these beings are capable of washing away some of the fluidic impurities clinging to him. Yes, it is a good practice to immerse yourself in water, but what is important is to be aware of the power it possesses. And if it has been blessed and magnetized, if an Initiate has pronounced certain formulas over it to consecrate it, it can be extremely efficacious. But even in this case, its power cannot last for ever. The effects of a rite of purification can only last if the person who has been purified or exorcized maintains his state of purity by the quality of his thoughts, feelings and actions ; if this is the case, and only if this is the case, then the purification will be lasting. In the spiritual life, external means have no lasting effect if the person who uses them does not live a pure, intelligent life. But as this is never explained to them, people cherish all kinds of illusions.

Let me give you another example : many Christians wear a cross or crucifix round their necks as a reminder that Jesus sacrificed his life for their salvation. They believe that it will protect them from illness and their own weaknesses. But, then, why are they always in such a pitiful state ? Why doesn't their cross save them ? Because for the cross to be magically efficacious and beneficial it has to be worn inwardly, in the form of a quality, virtue or power. You can wear a cross of gold or ivory or any other precious material but, however valuable it may be, if you wear it only outwardly, it can do nothing to help you. But if you magnetize a cross and steep it in your own faith and love, and use it as a means to strengthen your ties with Christ, then yes, it can be extraordinarily powerful.

A cross can only save you if your spirit participates fully in the wearing of it, and if you live in conscious communication with light, with Christ. You have to adhere to the principle hidden behind the form of the cross so as to understand its meaning and strive to put it into practice. Keep certain forms, if you like, but be sure never to lose sight of the spirit concealed behind them. For me, the cross is the most fantastic symbol... Yes, particularly a three-dimensional cross, formed of five cubes whose twenty-two facets correspond to the twenty-two letters of the Cabbalah with which God created the world.

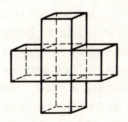

Christians can wear crosses and medals, burn candles and recite rosaries as much as they like, but as long as they do nothing to put life into these objects they will remain ineffective. In fact it all becomes rather ridiculous ! It is time they stopped relying on dead things and realized that it is up to them to put life into them.

One day, people will begin to realize that there is no point in priding oneself on having been baptized a Catholic, for that is not enough. One has to work consciously, all one's life, to *become* a Catholic. When a child is only a few days old, long before it can have an opinion on the subject, it is baptized as a Catholic ; later on it may well prefer to be a Muhammadan, a Taoist, a Jew or a Buddhist ! Don't be scandalized by what I am saying : try to understand that I am simply trying to get you to broaden your point of view. It is all very well to have been baptized Catholic, Protestant, Anglican or Orthodox, but is the life you are living really divine ? Is it the life of an Angel ? No, you are living a life that is half-way between that of an animal and that of a human being.

So stop being so sure that, since you have been baptized, you can sit back and do nothing more. A Catholic should tell himself : 'Every day I must consciously strive to become catholic, that is to say, universal. There must be no room in my heart any longer for divisiveness, hatred, resentment or hostility, only for the overriding conviction that all men are children of God.' But you still feel that the faithful of other religions are not God's children and that you must reject them. Well, it is precisely in this that you are not catholic ! If you were truly catholic, you would embrace all human beings, even if their opinions differed from yours in every respect, because you would know that they are your brothers and sisters, sons and daughters of God.

4

THE ADVENT
OF THE CHURCH OF ST. JOHN

Each religion has set aside a day of the week for worship, which differs from one religion to the next : for Christians it is Sunday, for Jews it is Saturday, for Muhammadans, Friday, and so on. But is there any real difference, actually, between the different days of the week ? No, none at all ! Every day is sacred, every day is divine. Friday is a day for doing good ; Saturday is a day for doing good, and Sunday is a day for doing good ! In the Universal White Brotherhood every day of the week is holy. What would it be like if only one day in the week were holy ? You could forget the Lord and break all His laws for six days a week and on the seventh, you would go to church and try to wipe out the stains of the sins committed during the week ! No, you cannot purify yourself in just one day ; you need every day of the week for that. If you think of God only once a week, and forget Him all the rest of the time, because you are too busy with your shady business deals, your rivalries or your adulterous love affairs... Why, it is simply grotesque ! It is nothing but lies and hypocrisy ! What really counts is how you live on the six other days.

In the new religion it will seem too little to devote only a few hours or a single day to prayer and church-going. We must be in God's church every day and all day, for God's church is the whole of creation. Oh, I know very well that one cannot expect a great deal of human beings who are still so raw and hard-headed. For many, one whole day is already too much to ask ! But when the new religion comes, human beings will want to be mystical seven days a week ; they will try to be pure seven days a week ; they will pray and cultivate good thoughts seven days a week. And when those seven days are over, they will begin again for another seven days... And so on, for the rest of their lives ! In fact, isn't that what we are doing here, at the Bonfin ? Here, every day is Sunday — or Saturday or Friday, if you prefer — and we spend the whole day in church. What church ? The church that is outside us, all round us : the whole of nature, but, most especially, the church that is within, for each one of us is a temple of the Living God.

You have read, in St. John's Gospel, what Jesus replied to the Samaritan woman at the well. She said : 'Our fathers worshipped on this mountain, and you Jews say that in Jerusalem is the place where one ought to worship.' And Jesus replied : 'Woman, believe me, the hour is coming when you will worship the Father neither on this mountain, nor in Jerusalem... But the hour is coming, and now is, when the true worshippers will worship the Father in spirit and truth.' But as the time had not yet come to teach these truths to the masses, Jesus could not give his disciples the philosophical, cabbalistic, esoteric (or, if you prefer, symbolic) foundations on which these new notions were based. This is why he chose St. John and, without telling the other apostles, prepared him in secret. But the others saw this and they were a little jealous ; on one occasion, in fact, St. Peter even reproached Jesus for it. But Jesus was anxious to entrust to at least one of his disciples those parts of his teaching that were still unrevealed. That was why he prepared St. John, and St. John founded a Church which has never really been accepted or understood by the Church of St. Peter.

You remember what Jesus said to St. Peter the last time he appeared to his disciples after his resurrection. Peter, seeing John, said to Jesus : 'But, Lord, what about this man ?' Jesus said to him, 'If I will that he remain till I come, what is that to you ?' And the Gospel adds : 'Then this saying went out among the brethren that this disciple would not die.' And now, suppose that St. John were still living in some secret place ! In the course of the centuries, His Church has prepared an elite body of men to whom Esoteric Science has been entrusted. Take just one example : is the Church of Peter capable of interpreting the symbols contained in the Book of Revelation ? Do you know that I have even heard priests saying that St. John must have lost the use of his faculties as he grew older, otherwise he would never have written anything so extravagant ! But it is the Church of St. John which is going to manifest itself one day. It will not make any difference what the Catholic, Protestant and Orthodox Churches do to try and stop it. They have already done all they could, in the past, to exterminate the Church of St. John without success. And they will not succeed in the future, any more than they succeeded in the past.

All the most exalted spirits of Christendom, all those who stood out as examples of purity and wisdom, were disciples of St. John, and the others, those of the official Church, who were jealous of their superiority, never stopped persecuting them. But that Church, which has always been forced to live and work in secret, continues to instruct the sons and daughters of God, and now, in our day, it is going to come out into the open and reveal itself before all men and manifest its superiority, its spiritual wealth and its universality. When this day comes, whether it likes it or not, the Church of Peter will be obliged to change and to introduce some reforms. Of course, I don't deny that there is a minority of elite souls in the Church of Peter, but what about all the others ? I would not like to tell you what they are interested in ! Instead of being ready to learn and try to improve themselves, they have always been content to persecute anyone who was better than them.

The Church of St. Peter has always been extremely intolerant, persecuting and burning anyone who refused to think or behave exactly as she ordered them. Whereas the members of the Church of St. John have never persecuted anyone ; they have always left each person free to do as he pleased, for they were only interested in perfecting themselves, in trying to attain their ideal of divine perfection. They have never had any earthly ambitions. The Church of Peter, on the contrary, has always tried to dominate others and impose its own rules. In fact, it was in order to do this that it kept human beings for so long in a state of mediocrity and helplessness. 'Seek perfection ? But that's pride ! It's the Devil who has put that idea into your head !' And yet, didn't Jesus say, 'You shall be perfect, just as your Father in heaven is perfect.' This is the highest ideal there is, and if others have a different ideal... well, that's their business !

Don't think that I'm trying to destroy the Church : certainly not ! On the contrary, I am ready to collaborate with the Church by giving it the light that is lacking to it at the moment. Actually, I have already tried : I have talked to priests and monks, but never with any success. Well, I should say that I have had some success with a few, but there is nothing one can do for most of them. Their training in the seminary was so successful in drumming the conviction into their heads that Catholicism was the only true religion, that their minds are deformed : they are stuck fast, incapable of going a step further. That is why I much prefer to deal with atheists and unbelievers : we understand each other more easily. But people who have strong religious convictions : what a problem they are ! They are so bigoted and narrow-minded ! Oh, I am sure that all this will change one day, but only after all kinds of tribulations which will oblige them to think again.

In the Book of Revelation, St. John speaks of 'a new heaven and a new earth'. What does that mean ? Have the first heaven and earth grown old ? If so, the Lord must have used materials that were not of the very best quality, and that does not say much for Him, does it ? It means that He is not omniscient after all ! No, the truth is that the 'new heaven and new earth' apply to us, to our inner life. In the language of Initiates, which is the language of eternal symbols, 'a new heaven' means new ideas and perceptions, a new understanding, a new philosophy. And a 'new earth' means new attitudes, a new behaviour. So a 'new heaven and a new earth' are a new mentality and a new way of life. 'Heaven' represents the head, the mind, and 'the earth' represents the feet. The feet walk in the direction indicated by the head ; they go wherever the head leads them, into terrain that it has already explored. In other words, man's behaviour, the things he does and the way he does them, will change in keeping with the changed head, in keeping with the new way of looking at things, the new philosophy.

But is this new heaven that God is creating really new ? No, not really : it has been there for all eternity, but to human beings, it will be new. It has always been there, it is waiting for them, but they have never seen it, and one day, when they suddenly discover it, it will be new to them. So 'a new heaven and a new earth' means that human beings will rise to greater heights and that, there, they will discover something that has always existed in God's plans for them, but which they had never glimpsed before. The situation is exactly the same in what concerns man's attitude towards the sun : the sun has always been there, but man has still not understood how essential it is in his life. As long as we have not learned to rejoice in its presence, as long as we do not contemplate it as it rises, as long as we have still not experienced the yearning to resemble it, we have still not discovered it. We are still in the outdated, moth-eaten, decaying heaven of the past ![1]

The 'new earth' is a new way of behaving, a new way of doing things. But this new behaviour is only possible if the 'new heaven' is already in place. And this 'new heaven' is the sun, our understanding of all that the sun teaches us, of all the riches it gives us in its light, heat and life. It is the sun that will open our eyes to the 'new heaven' in which dwell the Angels, Archangels and Divinities... this heavenly dwelling which Jesus called 'My father's house'.

And you, too, can dwell in this new heaven already, today and every day. As soon as you accept the new philosophy of those sublime beings who came to enlighten mankind, you dwell already in this new heaven. And once you get to know the new heaven, the new philosophy, you will be obliged to change your behaviour, your way of doing things. All the methods that you are learning here with regard to nutrition, breathing, words and gestures : all this is the new earth.

A new light is dawning, my dear brothers and sisters, and it will create such harmony and unity amongst men that the whole earth will be one family, and brotherliness and peace will reign throughout the world.

1 See *Complete Works*, vol. 10, chap. 13 ; also *Toward a Solar Civilization*, Collection Izvor, N° 201 A, chap. 8.

5

THE FOUNDATIONS
OF A UNIVERSAL RELIGION

All religions have a tendency to emphasize certain truths which, admittedly, are essential, but which are taught to the exclusion of others which are equally essential. Religions are like medicines which can only cure certain types of infection : as they only teach part of the truth, they are not capable of answering all the needs of the human soul and spirit. If a religion aspires to being universal, it must teach the truths contained in all religions and philosophies, and be able to provide all men with the spiritual work best suited to each one. This is what our Teaching does.

Everything that can help men to be closer to God and to understand the mysteries of the universe is contained in our Teaching. And this includes not only the great truths taught by Christianity, but also the Jewish cabbalistic system, the science of purity and the two principles of the Persians, the solar religion of Egypt, the philosophy of immortality of the Chinese, the methods of meditation and breathing and the various yogas of India, the science of the magi, alchemists and astrologers, etc., etc. A universal religion must teach human beings all the great truths of Initiatic Science.

So, if I say that the world needs a universal religion, it is because Catholicism is not yet universal. Oh, I know that the word 'catholic' means universal, but in spite of that, the Catholic religion is not really universal. The fact that it has rejected many essential truths such as reincarnation, the laws of Karma and the importance of the sun in the spiritual life, means that it has cut itself off from some universal truths : it, too, is a sect. I am very sorry if some of you are offended by what I am saying but, after all, the important thing is to know what truly exists in reality, not whether that reality pleases or displeases some.

A universal religion must encompass all the knowledge and all the practices that enable man to reach God. When Christianity refuses to teach reincarnation it is preventing men from understanding God's justice. No wonder, then, if all the rest becomes absurd : if you cannot see the underlying reason for things, they seem arbitrary and unjust. In the face of evil or suffering, a Christian can only say, 'It is the will of God.' It is never the fault of the person who is suffering, God forbid ! He has never done anything to bring misfortune on himself. You cannot blame him, he is innocent ! It is the

Lord who is responsible. But this means that God is capricious and cruelly unjust. He does whatever He pleases !

By denying reincarnation, Christians have put up road-blocks to their own progress that have lasted for centuries. Whereas, when you accept reincarnation, everything falls into place : you know that certain causes produce certain effects from one life to the next, and you cannot blame God for any of it : it is we, ourselves, who are responsible. It is we who choose this path or that manifestation ; it is we who determine our own destiny, not God. God remains untouched and unsullied in His grandeur and splendour, in His true perfection and justice. Whereas, when we deny reincarnation, all the blame for our misfortunes falls on Him. It seems to me that if Christians were more concerned with the glory and perfection of God they would accept reincarnation. But they have such a narrow view that they don't even realize the consequences of their attitude ; they cannot see what a horrifying idea of God they project. They should not be surprised if most people, today, are turning away from religion.

As long as the Church continues to deny reincarnation it is portraying the Lord as a monster and a tyrant. As a matter of fact, I could say quite a lot about the notion Christianity has of God, for it inherited the Old Testament image of God as a jealous, vindictive, despotic God who was always punishing and chastising human beings. In spite of what Jesus taught, the God of Christians is still the God of Moses.

You may object that reincarnation was never mentioned in the Gospels. Actually, it was, but you don't know how to read the Gospels. Let me give you some arguments that I have already spoken of in the past.

The Gospels tell us how, when Jesus learned that John the Baptist had been arrested, he departed to Galilee, and not long after, John was beheaded by order of Herod. After the Transfiguration the disciples asked Jesus, 'Why do the scribes say that Elijah must come first ?' and Jesus replied, 'Elijah truly is coming first and will restore all things. But I say to you that Elijah has come already, and they did not know him but did to him whatever they wished.' And the text adds, 'Then the disciples understood that he spoke to them of John the Baptist.'

And now let's look at the life of the Prophet Elijah ; it will help us to understand why he was beheaded when he reincarnated as St. John the Baptist. Elijah lived at the time of King Ahab who was married to Jezebel, a foreign princess, daughter of the king of Sidon, and, because of her influence, Ahab worshipped her foreign gods, Baal and Ashtoreth. Elijah came before Ahab and reproached him for being unfaithful to the true God. Then he told him, 'There shall not be dew nor rain these years, except at my word.' Then Elijah went and hid in the mountains to escape the wrath of Ahab.

Three years went by and the country was ravaged by drought. So, once again, God sent Elijah to Ahab. When the king saw the Prophet he reproached him bitterly : 'Is that you, O troubler of Israel ?' And Elijah replied, 'I have not troubled Israel, but you and your father's house have, in that you have forsaken the commandments of the Lord, and you have followed the Baals. Now therefore, send and gather all Israel to me on Mount Carmel and the four hundred and fifty prophets of Baal...' So all the prophets were assembled, and Elijah said, 'Let them give us two bulls ; and let them choose one bull for themselves... and lay it on the wood... and I will prepare the other bull and lay it on the wood. Then you call on the name of your gods, and I will call on the name of the Lord ; and the God who answers by fire, he is God.'

Then from early in the morning the prophets of Baal, began their invocations : 'O Baal, Baal, hear us !' But there was no response, and Elijah jeered at them, saying : 'Cry aloud, for he is a god ; either he is meditating, or he is busy, or he is on a journey, or perhaps he is sleeping and must be awakened.' So the prophets cried all the louder and tried to practise magic by slashing their bodies with knives, hoping that their blood would attract evil spirits and elementals who would bring down fire on their altar. But, although they continued like that all day, nothing happened.

Then Elijah said, 'That is enough ! Bring me twelve stones.' With the stones he built an altar and round the altar he made a trench ; then he piled wood on the stones and cut the bull in pieces, and laid it on the wood. Then Elijah told the people to pour water over the whole thing and to fill the trench with water. When it had all been done as he said, Elijah called on the Lord, saying, 'Lord God of Abraham, Isaac, and Israel, let it be known this day that You are God in Israel, and that I am Your servant, and that I have done all these things at Your word.' Then fire fell from Heaven and consumed everything : the victim, the wood and even the stones and the water. When the people saw this, they fell to their knees and acknowledged that the God of Elijah was the true God. But then Elijah, who was a little too proud of his triumph, ordered the four hundred and fifty prophets of Baal to be taken to a brook where their throats were to be slit.

So you can see why it was only to be expected that his turn would come to have his head cut off, too. For there is a law, the law that Jesus referred to in the Garden of Gethsemane when he rebuked Peter for cutting off the ear of the High Priest's servant, saying : 'Peter, put your sword in its place, for all who take the sword will perish by the sword.'

Now, we know that this law does not always make itself felt at once. For Elijah, in fact, not only escaped assassination, but we are told that he was still alive when he was carried up to Heaven in a chariot of fire ! It was only later, when he returned as John the Baptist, that his sin was punished. Jesus knew who John was and the fate that awaited him, and this is why he did nothing to save him from it, although he praised him very highly, saying, 'Among those born of women there has not risen one greater than John the Baptist.' Justice had to be done.

Let's take another example from the Gospels. One day Jesus and his disciples met a man who was blind from birth and the disciples asked, 'Rabbi, who sinned, this man or his parents, that he was born blind ?' Do you think that anyone who did not believe in reincarnation would ask a question like that ? How could he have sinned before birth ? In his mother's womb ? Either it is a ridiculous question or it implies belief in a previous life. Perhaps you will object that Jesus' disciples were uneducated men and that they might well have asked some very stupid questions. But if this had been so, wouldn't Jesus have pointed that out to them ? The Gospels mention several occasions when Jesus reprimanded his disciples, but this is not one of them.

Some of you will, perhaps, think that if Jesus and his disciples believed in reincarnation, one would expect to find the word, at least once, in the Gospels. But there is really no reason to be surprised that the authors of the Gospels did not mention reincarnation explicitly at a time when, after all, everyone believed in it. How were they to guess that they should mention it in preparation for an era when human beings would have become so estranged from Initiatic Science ? All things considered, they said very little in their writings ; they were not going to waste time explaining something that already belonged to their tradition.

Let's take yet another passage in the Gospels : that in which Jesus says, 'You shall be perfect just as your Father in heaven is perfect.' How should we understand this phrase ? One is tempted to think either that Jesus spoke thoughtlessly when he asked creatures as limited as we are to attain the perfection of their Heavenly Father within the few short years of a lifetime, or that he had no notion of the greatness of God and imagined that it was easy to match His perfection. In either case it does not say much for Jesus ! But, of course, this phrase implies the fact of reincarnation. Jesus knew very well that man was incapable of becoming perfect in only one lifetime, but he also knew that if he aspired to perfection and worked to attain it, after many incarnations he would end by reaching his goal.

Then there is also this passage in Genesis : 'God said, ''Let Us make man in Our image, according to Our likeness''... So God created man in His own image ; in the image of God He created him'. What happened to the 'likeness' ?

Look at an acorn : it is in the image of its father, the oak tree, by which I mean that it contains the same potential to become a magnificent tree, but it is not 'like' its father yet ; it does not have the same shape or size, the same form ; it will only become like its father when it has been planted and had time to grow. And man is in the image of God : like God he is a trinity of wisdom, love and power. But these attributes in man are of a degree far, far inferior to those of his Creator, Who is all-wise, all-loving and all-powerful. [1] But one day, when man has grown to his full stature, he will be like God and will possess the fullness of His virtues. So you see that, here too, the evolution from 'image' to 'likeness' implies reincarnation. God said, 'Let Us make man in Our image, according to Our likeness' but He did not do so. 'God created man in His own image ; in the image of God He created him' : the notion of reincarnation is concealed in the fact that the word 'likeness' is missing and the word 'image' is repeated twice. Yes, there is considerable matter for thought, here.

1 See *Toward a Solar Civilization*, Collection Izvor, N° 201 A, chap. 10.

There is nothing to prevent the Catholic religion from boasting that it is universal if it wants to ; that is what it believes, but its belief is not shared by Initiates. A universal religion must be founded on the essential needs of human beings. And these are the same for all men. This is why the only religion that is universal is the solar religion, for everyone needs the sun, everyone seeks the sun and loves and understands it. Everything else concerns some men and not others, suits some but not others. Indeed, if there are so many different religions, it is because each one of them is adapted to a particular mentality. The religion of the future will be founded on universal elements which will be food and drink to all human beings. Whereas, nowadays, we see Christians becoming Buddhists or Muhammadans ; Jews or Muhammadans becoming Christians, and so on. In other words, no one religion is universal. When the universal religion comes, no one will feel the need to go looking elsewhere, all will be in the same religion.

Behind the sun is the God of all men. Christians don't need the Hindu gods, and Hindus don't need the God of Christians ; Muhammadans don't need the God of the Jews, and so forth, but they all need the sun which gives light, warmth and life to men, animals and plants. The Christian religion illuminates and warms only a few million people in the world — and who knows exactly where that light and warmth come from. But how many millions have never even heard of Christianity ! And, unfortunately for Christianity, they get on much better without it !

There are too many religions in the world. In fact, this is the cause of all the misfortunes of mankind. We only need one religion : the religion of light, warmth and life, the religion of the sun. Christians reject this idea on the pretext that we must adore and glorify God alone. But they are incapable of reaching God here and now, so, in the meantime, they are in a vacuum. They are so convinced that they must adore only God that they don't feel or understand anything about the spiritual life. Well, I ask you, is that intelligent ? Why cannot they see that only the sun can bring us closer to God, because it is the living image of His splendour, of His light, love and power ? They spurn the sun ? Very well, let them remain, cold and helpless, in darkness !

Humans are very strange creatures ! Their theologians love to invent all kinds of abstract theories about the Deity, using words like essence, substance and transcendence, and squabbling amongst themselves about all these theories, while the masses understand not a word of what they are saying ! But if you ask them to understand that the sun can catapult them all the way to God Himself... Ah, no ! They cannot accept that. Well, whether they like it or not the religion of the future is going to be the religion of the sun, because it is the sun that gives us the most faithful image of the Blessed Trinity. Don't misunderstand me : I am not saying that God is in the solar disc that we see shining in the sky. No, but I am saying that the sun, with its light, warmth and life which it distributes so generously throughout the universe, is the best image we can have of the wisdom, love and life of God.

The religion taught by Jesus was perfect ; I am not denying that. But it has been so deformed over the centuries, that nowadays it is an artificial culture-medium swarming with the germs of every kind of fermentation. It is essential to abandon all these various false conceptions and find the only true religion, the religion that has existed from the beginning of the universe and which will exist until the end.

It is time for men to turn to the universal principle which is the source of all religions, and learn to decipher the symbol of that universal religion : the sun. The religion of the sun can be summed up in the two words, 'give' and 'unite', for the sun illuminates, warms and gives life to all creatures. Before mankind even existed, the sun was already there. From the beginning of time he has been telling us : 'Do as I do ; give light, warmth and life to others, and shake off your narrow, limited conceptions. Let your intelligence and love embrace the whole world.'

The language of the sun is universal. Everyone can understand it. It is the language of light, warmth and life. Men, animals and plants all understand the language of the sun, whereas you can never be sure that they will understand other languages. Do you really think that all the tribes of Africa and the South Sea Islands have understood the Christian language ? And yet they have had many missionaries working amongst them. The cannibals who complained that they were starving because they had not had enough missionaries... do you think that they had understood the Christian language ?

True religion teaches that man must draw closer to the light, warmth and life of the sun. In other words, that he must seek the wisdom that can illuminate him and solve all problems, the disinterested love that encourages and consoles and makes everything it touches more beautiful, and the subtle, spiritual life that can make him active, dynamic and intrepid so that he becomes capable of establishing the Kingdom of God and His Righteousness on earth. And no one can fight against the new religion ; anyone who attempts to destroy it commits an act of self-destruction, because he is imposing limitations on himself.

Once this understanding of universal religion has penetrated the minds of men, every aspect of organized life will also become universal : human beings will no longer be separated, there will be no more national boundaries, no more war. It was not Nature — and certainly not God — that marked out frontiers and boundaries : it was the covetousness of man. The new philosophy, the new religion, teaches, first and foremost, that the earth belongs to no one but God. Is it a sign of intelligence and Christian love to fight over a piece of land ? The fact is that it is not possible to possess the earth : when we leave for the next world, the earth stays behind. We cannot take it with us ! So what good has it ever done to fight over it ?

We must stop trying to impose the point of view of one race or one religion on the rest of the world. We must all move forward together towards the universal religion and brotherhood that the sun teaches. The sun does not discriminate between different nationalities, races or religions : he gives his light, warmth and life to all men, Catholic, Protestant, Muhammadan and Buddhist alike. And we must be like him.

When I say that we are bringing a new religion, it does not mean that our Teaching is superior to that of Jesus. That is impossible ! There is nothing higher or more perfect than love, sacrifice, abnegation, light and purity. But the Gospels have not said it all ; if the Teaching of the Universal White Brotherhood is a step forward in relation to the Gospels, it is precisely on the level of explanations, methods and practical ways of applying Christ's Teaching.

And true Christians, Christians who are really sincere, cannot deny that this is the true religion of Christ. They cannot accuse our Teaching of spreading heresy or of being a sect.

The great founders of religions : Krishna, Buddha, Zoroaster, Orpheus, Pythagoras, Moses, Jesus, Muhammad and so on, all lived in one particular country. And this means that their teaching reached only a certain number of people. But Christ is a universal principle : it was He who manifested Himself through each of these great Masters. Even though Jesus is still at work with Christians in the invisible world, Buddha with Buddhists, Muhammad with Muhammadans, and so on, their action is limited ; whereas Christ is at work throughout the whole world, for He is a Cosmic Principle.

Christ belongs to no one people, race or religion. He is a solar spirit. But He is even more immense than the sun ; He manifests Himself far beyond our sun, throughout the immensity of the cosmos in which there are many, many suns, bigger and brighter than ours. And yet it is still our own sun that is our best route to Christ and our Heavenly Father. By getting to know the sun more intimately, in his sublime manifestations of light, heat and life, human beings will also come closer and closer to the Deity, and the earth will become a Garden of Eden where all men will live together as brothers.

6

THE GREAT
UNIVERSAL WHITE BROTHERHOOD

The different reigns of nature with all the creatures that belong to each reign, are all linked together. Although we may not know it, we have ties with all beings that exist both on the higher planes above and on the levels below ours. In other words, there is a hierarchy of life in nature, and it is thanks to this hierarchy, thanks to our ties with a higher order of beings, that we, ourselves, can rise to higher planes. And it is also thanks to this hierarchy that we have ties with the lower reigns of nature : animals, plants and even the stones.

Man believes himself to be alone, but in fact he is linked to millions of other beings, and he can communicate with them by means of his thoughts and feelings. If his thoughts and feelings are good, noble and luminous they have a beneficial influence on the beings who are below him on the hierarchical scale, while, at the same time, they trigger certain effects in the higher reigns of being, and divine energies begin to flow into him.

Wisdom and light and the love of Angels, Arch-angels and divinities flow through Initiates and the great Masters, and reach every human being that is capable of receiving them. But these forces do not stop there ; they flow on through human be-ings, down to the animal, vegetable and mineral reigns. Then they begin to rise again on another, upward current, from the level of minerals, up to the highest levels of creation, in a prodigious flow of energies that courses through the whole universe.

Every link in this living chain of creatures is traversed by the joy, peace and light of higher be-ings. If you decide to remain separate, alone and independent, you are putting yourself in great danger, because you are depriving yourself of the possibility of drawing on these beneficial currents, and if you do this where will your inspiration come from ? Where will you get the strength you need to live each day ? 'We'll find it in ourselves', you will say. Yes, perhaps ; for a month or two, or even a year. But you will soon use up your reserves. If pride and the desire for independence leads you to break the bonds that bind you to the higher planes, your strength will slip away from you. Even if you start out with a lot of grand and noble schemes, in a very short time there will be nothing left of them, for it is impossible to accomplish anything of any importance without that link with the living chain of creation. It is exactly as though an electric light bulb prided itself on producing light, without realizing that it is simply a conductor of the current that comes from the central powerhouse.

The truth is that, whether we like it or not, we are all linked, connected to each other. But it is important to be conscious of our link with entities of a higher order, so that the living current can flow through us. If you refuse or neglect to establish this conscious bond, sooner or later you will lose your light and strength and all the other qualities you may possess. Man is capable of great power ; he is capable of performing miracles, but he must never forget that he is simply a conductor of energies from above. He must remember to tell himself, 'It is Divine Wisdom that is acting in me... The Divine World is manifesting itself through my actions.' If he fails to remember this he will lose everything.

Brotherhood must be established on earth, amongst all men, for it already exists in the universe. It is this that we call the Great Universal White Brotherhood, and it encompasses all the Saints, Prophets, Initiates and great Masters of mankind. And Christ is its head.

The Universal White Brotherhood is a power which extends to the limits of the solar system and beyond. You must not make the mistake of judging it by the Brotherhood that exists here, on earth : a handful of men and women who are not always very wise or enlightened. The true Universal White

Brotherhood on high is composed of all the most highly evolved beings that have ever existed, whereas we are simply workers who are trying to benefit from the light and support of those beings in order to carry out their plans on earth. But the Brotherhood on earth must become a faithful reflection of the one on high ; and this means that its members must become more and more keenly aware of the tremendous privilege they have received in belonging to this sublime entity.

Even you have still not really understood what it means to be a member of the Universal White Brotherhood. Some of you complain that nothing has really changed in their lives since they started to follow this Teaching. This is because they are present outwardly, physically, but not inwardly. When a disciple is inwardly a member of the Universal White Brotherhood, he cannot help but evolve and become stronger and richer. As long as someone is content to rub along in this little Brotherhood on earth, with all those who congregate here because they don't know what else to do with themselves, naturally, he will not gain from it : nothing can ever be gained by purely external means. But if he belongs, with all his heart and soul, to the Great Universal White Brotherhood on high, and if he works to carry out its plans here on earth, then his life will be changed.

When I speak of the Universal White Brotherhood, I am not referring to you, the little group of men and women who are members of the Brotherhood on earth, but to that sublime assembly on high which is the source of our light and strength. This is why, if you want to be invulnerable, you must never leave the powerful, indestructible fortress of the Universal White Brotherhood. Within the walls of this enclosure of light, you are invulnerable ; hostile forces draw back and make way for you. But once you leave it, you are lost ! It does not matter in the least if you leave Izgrev or the Bonfin[1] or any other centre of the Brotherhood, as long as your link with the Brotherhood on high remains intact. But once you have left the Brotherhood inwardly, no one is going to gain anything if you stay here physically — least of all yourself.

What is the use of having a car in the garage if there is no one to drive it ? It is not the car that matters, but the driver, that is to say, the spirit of man. Unfortunately, there are a lot of 'cars' in the Brotherhood without drivers. Where are their drivers ? Drinking and amusing themselves in a bar or a night-club — symbolically speaking ! Do you really think that all those who come here, are truly

1 Izgrev is the administrative headquarters of the Universal White Brotherhood, in Sèvres, just outside Paris. The Bonfin is the Brotherhood's principal convention centre, at Fréjus on the French Riviera.

here ? It is impossible to tell where they really are...
But when you are all here together, truly present
in mind and body, soul and spirit, extremely powerful invisible currents are set in motion, and these
currents attract luminous spirits of the invisible
world who come and join with us and bring us their
blessings.

All your failures and misfortunes come from the
fact that you cut yourselves off from the chain of
the Great Universal White Brotherhood. This is why
it is so important for you to think of this chain and
tune in to its harmonious vibrations every single day,
if only for a few minutes. If you do this, all the
freedom, bliss and ecstasy experienced and enjoyed
by these higher entities, all the treasures and pearls
of great price that they possess, will become yours.
Yes, for Initiates and great Masters are not interested in keeping their treasures for themselves,
they immediately hand them on to those below, and
if you are not receiving them it is because you have
set yourselves apart from that living chain of beings : you have made yourselves incapable of receiving them.

If a disciple fails to maintain his ties with the
Universal White Brotherhood, it can have very dire
consequences for him : as the currents from above
no longer flow through him, there is nothing to
sweep toxic elements out of his system and purify
him. And when this happens, swarms of inferior

beings are attracted by the impurities that accumulate, and start slipping in and creating havoc in his interior. When you feel that you are being invaded by creatures who are trampling all over your inner flower beds, stealing your treasures and putting out your lights, it means that you have failed to keep contact with the current of the Universal White Brotherhood. And then you complain that you don't know what is happening to you, that you feel miserable, anxious and tormented, and you go and see a doctor or try to forget your problems in a whirl of activity... but to no avail ! The only way of getting rid of the inferior creatures that you are infested with is to restore your ties with the sublime world on high. You have to open your heart and mind, your soul and spirit to the beings of that world, so that blessings from above can, once again, flow into you and purify and nourish you and rescue you from the malignant invaders. When the current from above is very powerful, creatures from the lower world cannot swim against it, it pushes them back. But if they have managed to get a foothold within you, it means that you have broken or weakened your ties with the Great Universal White Brotherhood, and the current from above was not strong enough to keep them out.

The Great Universal White Brotherhood is the only safe stronghold, believe me ! Those who aspire to being members must beg the sublime entities on high to accept them ; if need be, I shall intervene in their favour. I shall explain, 'These are my children ; open your doors to them. Yes, they still cling to many old attachments from the past, but they are full of goodwill, and life is very hard for some of them ! Please give them a chance.' And as our friends in the invisible world are very wealthy, they ask nothing better than to distribute some of that wealth.

7

FOR A UNIVERSAL NOTION
OF THE FAMILY

I want to talk to you, today, about a notion which, I am well aware, will not be well received either by your hearts or your minds. No, because, instead of making an honest effort to understand that I am trying to lead you to a much more elevated point of view, you are going to react according to your old conceptions and traditions, and what I have to say will arouse your indignation. Let me tell you in advance that I am sorry that this is so, but I must still say what I have to say, for I have to prepare the ground. So try to listen carefully until I have finished ; perhaps you will understand the advantages of what I am going to say.

For thousands of years the family has always been considered the basic unit of human society. It is true that, within the last few decades, in Western society, the family has begun to disintegrate. But, in spite of everything, the family unit is still very important. Every human being lives in his family ; he loves it, works for it, protects and defends it. That is all very good, and it is normal ; I have no quarrel with that.

The family is a creation of Nature herself. Cosmic Intelligence saw that this way of life would be good for human beings because, in this way, they could help and support each other, work together and come to each other's defence. The family is like a stronghold, a solid, stable shelter in which the individual can feel safe. In the past, some families formed whole tribes ; in fact, they even declared war amongst themselves, as in the family vendettas in Corsica, for example !

So it is Nature that gives members of the same family this bond of affection, this need to be together to help and defend each other. And you can see the same thing with animals. But then we have to ask whether Cosmic Intelligence meant this situation to last for ever. Would it not be possible for human beings to go a step further ? Is it not possible for the form in which families were first created to be made broader and more noble and luminous ? It is time that men began to understand that the family, as we now think of it, is preventing mankind from forming a single unit, a single immense family. Why ? Because each little family is only interested in its own happiness and satisfaction, its own individual advantage, and this makes it impossible for its members to devote themselves to the larger Family of mankind.

This narrow conception of the family, therefore, is the source of all our limitations and all our self-centred enterprises, and it is time, now, for human beings to reach a broader outlook, to understand that all families must melt into the larger Family, otherwise the world will continue to see nothing but little clans at war with each other. Disorder and anarchy exist in the world because of this mentality which considers nothing greater or more important than the little family unit. Everybody thinks that it is so marvellous that it must, obviously, be encouraged. You only have to think of the advice that so many parents give their children : wangle things to your own advantage whenever you can ; cheat and fraud when necessary ; oust anyone who gets in your way ; succeed whatever the cost ! They never dream of inculcating a divine ideal into their children's minds, only the most selfish and egotistical ambitions. From time to time children are told that they must show love, generosity and forbearance in dealing with their brothers and sisters, but one does not see too much evidence of these virtues. Even members of the same family are constantly at each other's throats !

One often hears it said that the family is the basic cell of human society. That is true, but how do the cells of a human body function ? They all work and collaborate with each other for the good of the whole body. And is that what we see in society ? Not a bit of it : each family is apart and distinct from all the others, even when they are not actually rivals ! Each one has different ideas, different plans and different intentions which are a constant source of disturbances and disorders of every kind. It is high time we went a step further, and adopted a much broader understanding ; all families must melt into the one great Family, the universal Family. This does not mean that they have to disintegrate and disappear, no ; but they must join together in the service of a goal that is greater than them all. Just as all the minute cells of our bodies are united in their work for the health and well-being of the immense cell that a human being represents, so all individual families in the world must work together for the health and well-being of the whole body of mankind.

When I say that it is the spiritual dimension that must be given first place, this is what I am speaking about : the human collectivity, the great Family, universal brotherhood. And the little family unit must take second place. As long as men give priority to the little family, nothing will get any better. This is why you must not be afraid to replace certain conceptions if they have become too narrow or obsolete and erroneous. There is no danger of the family disappearing ; there is no question of wanting to abolish it ! But it must be allowed to burst its bonds and expand ; it has got to take its place in the larger Family, and then we shall see the triumph of the Kingdom of God and His Righteousness, the dawning of the Golden Age.

I am not against the family ; on the contrary, I admire it and I, too, have a family. The family is necessary, but that does not mean that everything else has to be sacrificed to it, for it is not the greatest or most important thing that exists. In fact, I shall go even further and say that the mission of the family is to help its members to become members of the great universal Family. This is what I want to get you to understand : the importance of the great Family, of that universal fraternal community for which every single member must work. So far the family has failed its mission, and that is why it is crumbling. How many families do you know that live in real harmony together ? Look at the number of divorces... The statistics speak for themselves. Is all that my fault ? I did not have anything to do with it. Long before I said anything about it at all, a lot of other people had set out to destroy the family !

If we want to save the family, our conception of it is going to have to be broadened ; it is going to have to encompass the whole world ; the whole

of humanity must become one family. Don't misunderstand me : I am not saying that you must no
longer look after the members of your own family.
You still have to feed and house them, earn money
for them and give them an education. But if you
do this with the expanded awareness I am talking
about, you will do it even better than before. You
will explain to them that it is by working for that
universal Family that they will solve their problems.
So far, the family has certainly never managed
to prevent misfortune, war and poverty in the world.
And all that will continue unless all the little families blend to form one great Family ; then it will
be finished : there will be no more war, no more
poverty.

The solution, the only real solution, is to be
found in the expansion of the notion of family. As
long as you are only interested in the welfare of your
own little family circle, you will never be in a position to contribute to that of the whole world :
whatever you do will be done only for your own
benefit — although, as a matter of fact, it is very
doubtful whether you will actually do yourself any
good. The Lord only knows whether, when you are
busy looking after your own interests, you are really
benefiting yourself ! But one thing is certain, and
that is that when you work to bring all families
together in the one great Family, you are working
not only for others, but also for yourself. For if this

idea becomes reality, a great many things in the world will improve and those improvements will benefit you, as well as everybody else. Otherwise you will never do any good to anyone, not even your own children, because with that kind of self-centred love, you are instilling notions into them that are far too personal. One day the spirits of your children will reproach you for failing them, for not teaching them divine ideas, for having retarded their evolution.

Children very often cause their parents great unhappiness because, quite unconsciously, they blame them for bringing them up with a mean, narrow mentality, instead of teaching them to walk the path of generosity and light. Oh yes, this whole question has far-reaching consequences ! Many people congratulate themselves on doing their duty and working for the good of their family. But, in fact, can they be sure that that is what they are doing ? If you judge their behaviour from a celestial point of view, you will be bound to recognize that they are content to maintain the members of their family in a narrow spirit of selfishness and obscurity, which means that they are not doing anyone any good. So, be careful ! Make an effort to change your point of view ; devote yourselves to working for the great Family and then everything in your own life will prosper. Human beings need spiritual nourishment, and if you are incapable of giving it to them, they will leave you. How many women have walked out on their husbands because they only looked after them on the material level and never gave them anything for the nourishment of their soul or spirit !

A great many parents complain that their children are leaving home and joining some of the sects that are springing up in such profusion nowadays. They cannot understand why, in spite of all their love and kindness and the sacrifices they have made for them, their children feel the need to go off and find another kind of 'family'. So they fly into a rage, set the police on their tracks, get themselves interviewed by journalists and make a lot of accusations which are often very unjust, in the hope of getting public opinion on their side. For, as everyone knows, if the family structure starts to disintegrate, if the family, which is the foundation of all social life, begins to crumble, it is a serious and very dangerous situation ! Of course it is dangerous ! And, of course, it is admirable to want to defend family life ! I quite agree ; in fact, I have been doing nothing but that all my life. But how should this be done ? And what notion of the family should we be defending ? This is what you should ask yourselves.

If psychologists and educators studied the question honestly from the philosophical, ethical and psychological points of view, they would find out why some children feel the need to leave their parents. It is because young people, today, need something that they cannot find in their families ; they need a much broader vision of life, something vaster, nobler and more just ; this is what they hope to find by joining a sect.

A great many children leave home because of the small-mindedness and lack of understanding of their parents, or because of a way of life that is too commonplace and primitive. It is true that young people need an ideal ; they have a thirst for beauty and light and spiritual values in their lives ; they long to discover the hidden aspects of things. They are attracted by mystery and the supernatural. And it is only too true, unfortunately, that there are individuals who take advantage of these tendencies to lure the young into their own nets, and make a fortune by passing themselves off as spiritual Masters, even though they have all the same vices and weaknesses as everyone else. They do not know that it is forbidden to assume the role of a Master if one has not been tried and chosen and mandated for the task by true Masters. But people are so ignorant and lacking in discernment that they will persecute a true Initiate and follow the first upstart who proclaims himself to be a prophet, a saviour or Christ Himself. What is truly amazing is that in spite of all the Christs in the world, humanity is still in such a pitiful state !

But now, to those who really want to defend and

protect the family, let me say this : as long as parents do nothing to make their lives more aesthetic and intelligent, nobler and much more open, as long as they make no effort to be models of perfection for their children to follow, their children will continue to have only one idea in their heads : to leave home as soon as possible. It is not enough to feed and clothe your child and send him to school. You must give him something to nourish his heart and soul.

Let this idea of universality guide you in everything you do ; in this way you will benefit your family. In fact, if you enlighten many people and help them to come closer to the Lord in this life, they will come and reward you for it in future incarnations. Because you must not think that we live for all eternity with the members of our present family. They make up our family only for this incarnation ; God knows where they will be after this ! When you come to think of it, after all, is it really worth sacrificing the things of eternity for the sake of a family who will be yours for only one lifetime ? What is really worthwhile is to have a family for eternity. That is what I am working for : to have a family for eternity... and I know that I shall get it !

The more you want to keep your family for yourself, for your own pleasure, the more surely you will lose it : they will leave you and never come back in future incarnations, because they will have too

many unhappy memories of life in your company !
Whereas I am trying to work with disinterestedness,
because in that way I shall always keep you with
me, even in future incarnations. I give you so much
that you will have to come and look for me to thank
me, even if I am on another planet ! Because what
I am trying to give you is far more than any ordinary
family can give you.

If you read the Gospels, you will see that Jesus
had the same conception of the family as mine. The
Gospels tell us that, one day, as Jesus was talking
to his disciples, 'his brothers and his mother came,
and standing outside they sent to him, calling him.
And a multitude was sitting round him : and they
said to him, "Look, your mother and your brothers
are outside seeking you." But he answered them,
saying, "Who is my mother, or my brothers ?" And
he looked round in a circle at those who sat about
him, and said, "Here are my mother and my
brothers ! For whoever does the will of God is my
brother and my sister and mother".' So for Jesus,
as you see, the real family includes all the children
of God, all the sons and daughters of God, wherever
they may be, on earth and even on the other planets.
This is the one immense family of God. And this
is why I, too, am in favour of the great Family.

The little family ? That's another matter. It is
altogether too possessive. And do you know why
everybody is so attached to their family ? You will

say, 'Because they love each other ; because of their affection for each other !' No, I don't believe it. It is because they are thinking of themselves ; they are thinking of their old age : they want to be sure of having the love and warmth of the family round them. It is all so egotistical ! By contrast, look at how animals behave : as soon as the young cub or fledgling is capable of looking after itself, its mother says, 'Out with you !' and pushes it out of the den or the nest. Animals are more disinterested than human beings : they never try to keep their young for themselves on the pretext that they love them ! Very often, parents who do that do not love their children at all, they are only thinking of themselves. Their attachment is nothing but self-interest or fear.

Now, in the light of what I have been saying, examine yourselves and analyse your conception of your family : what are your feelings towards it ? What are your plans for it ? What are your motives ? Try to see if it would not be to your advantage to look beyond the individual, personal aspect of the family and envisage it in its universal dimension. For the little family is nothing without the other family, the great Family. I know that what I am saying is diametrically opposed to some people's convictions and habits, but I cannot help that : I have to reveal the truth to you in order to help you to expand your consciousness of what is.

How many, many things there are, still, that need to be illuminated and corrected and straightened out. For thousands of years, so many false conceptions have been piling up, and now they stand in the way of man's happiness ! You only have to see how people behave : their lives are organized solely in view of their own survival : of having enough to eat and to wear, of earning their living, getting married and having children, etc. They only think about themselves. Oh, from time to time, of course, they do a little something for society, but most of the time, whatever they do is for themselves. And this is why the human condition never gets any better : because no one thinks of the collectivity ; everybody thinks only of himself and his family. People believe that if they organize their own lives well they will find the security they are looking for, but that is not so.

We all live in a collectivity, and if revolution, riots or war breaks out in that collectivity, our individual property will not be safe. So, even if we take a lot of trouble to make everything safe for ourselves, in point of fact we shall never be really safe, because the collectivity itself can explode and destroy everything. History witnesses to the fact that there is always a Sword of Damocles hanging over the head of every individual : there have been so many rich and powerful men who seemed to be invulnerable until, one day, strife broke out amongst the people, and they lost everything, even their lives ! This proves that the destiny of individual families is linked to that of the collectivity. If conditions in the collectivity are improved, therefore, each individual will be safe. Everything depends on the stability of the collectivity : this is the only guarantee of security and prosperity for the individual.

So there are two different ways of envisaging one's interests. The first is to think that we shall be sure of having all we need if we arrange our own lives without bothering about anyone else. But, as I have already pointed out, this is impossible : we are irrevocably tied to the collectivity, and when disaster strikes we cannot hope to escape ; we shall necessarily be caught up in the maelstrom, like everyone else. The other way of looking at things, the only right way, begins by doing all one can to improve conditions for the collectivity, since the well-being or the misfortune of each individual depends on that of the collectivity.

Yes, the only way really and truly to protect the family is to work for the world community. The leaders of every country in the world must understand that some form of world government is indispensable ; all the individual countries must become one country ; the whole world must become one family. You will say, 'You're asking the impossible !' and then you will tell me all the reasons why you think it is impossible ! But I know all that already. At the moment, to be sure, you are right : it is impossible. But I work for the future. In the future this unity will be achieved, because events will lead people to adopt this new way of looking at things. Disaster and war will make people change their outlook.

The time has come to accept the new philosophy that the Aquarian Age is bringing to the world. We must nourish and strengthen it by giving it more and more room in our hearts and minds, in our soul and spirit. The thoughts and feelings of all the enlightened beings in the world form a powerful light which is spreading and influencing the minds of men and women and, one day, the whole world will be touched and contaminated by this new light. This is why, as I have always said, when men are unaware of the fact that thought is an active force, their evolution is seriously hampered. But we know how powerful thought, meditation and prayer are, we know how beneficial their effects on mankind can be, and thanks to this knowledge we can participate in this great work of light so that the ideal of the Universal White Brotherhood may be disseminated throughout the world. And the Universal White Brotherhood desires only one thing : that the whole world be united in one family.

All religions believe that human beings are all children of the same Father. Yes, they believe... they believe ! But what use is belief, since they go on behaving as though they believed in nothing ? Even Christians, whose special prayer begins with the words, 'Our Father who art in heaven...', and who insist so much on the brotherly love that should unite all men... Look at how they behave amongst themselves ! Go to a Court of Law one day, and you will see if they behave like brothers and sisters ! They fly in the face of every precept given in the Gospels, division and destruction is rife between their countries and their Churches and even amongst members of the same family ! What conclusion can we draw ?

The Universal White Brotherhood is accomplishing a tremendous work in the world. The results are not very visible yet, but before long, I assure you, they will begin to be seen ; everybody will begin to speak the same language. So, is it such a bad thing to have some part in this work ? You should be proud, you know, to be able to say, 'My life has meaning now because I am working for the whole world !' But people prefer to go on with their insipid, insignificant little lives, instead of collaborating in such immense and glorious work and being of some use to others. 'Yes,' you will say ; 'But the trouble is that you can't see what you're doing.' Well, perhaps it cannot be seen, but it can be felt !

I am inviting you to collaborate in activities thanks to which you will feel your life becoming so interesting and so luminous that it will astonish you. You must understand that glory, true glory, true power and true happiness can only be found in this idea, this desire to accomplish a divine work for the whole world, for when you do this, you set in motion higher powers which come to visit you. And while you are here you can enjoy all the right conditions for this work : the philosophy, the living conditions, the environment, the ambience. What more do you want ? What are you waiting for ? When it comes to taking part in a fight, everybody is ready at once, but when you are asked to take part in a work for Heaven... Oh no, not on your life !

Now I have to tell you that this prodigious work that remains to be done here, on earth, has already been decided and decreed from above. Heaven has decided that all our human values are going to have to be changed. The only thing is that Heaven cannot intervene directly on earth, for the intermediary regions are like zones closed off from each other. It is not that they are really separated from each other, but as the matter of which each region is made is of a different density, nothing can be accomplished in any of them without the appropriate instruments. The spirits of the invisible world are extremely powerful, but they cannot act effectively on the physical plane, because they are not made of physical matter. In a spiritualistic seance it is the medium who provides the fluidic matter known as ectoplasm. Without this matter, the spirits cannot manifest themselves ; they could not move even a feather. But once they have it, they are capable, in an instant, of demolishing a house !

In the same way, the most exalted spirits of the divine world cannot intervene in human affairs unless human beings themselves give them the means to act. Picture to yourself a huge, solid fortress : unless there is a traitor who is willing to open the gates from within, the enemy could never enter. One day I remember I was talking to the Brotherhood, and I said, 'Do you know who I am ?' Well, of course, I had spoken in such portentous tones that everyone expected me to make some great revelation, and say, 'I am Jesus Christ or St. Paul or Tamerlane...', so they were very disappointed when I said, 'I am the traitor in your midst !' To be a traitor, after all, is not something to boast about ! But then I explained what I meant : 'The earth is a great fortress, so dark and impregnable that the Heavenly Hosts cannot enter it ; so there has to be a traitor to open the gates of this fortress to the forces of light and love, and that is my role.' Of course, once I had explained what I meant, they were all reassured and understood what I was saying.

The spirits above cannot do much on earth, for on earth it is human beings who are powerful, as powerful as all the armies of Heaven ; and when men decide to oppose them, there is not much they can do. This is why Heaven tries to find someone to open the doors and let them in. A truly spiritual person, therefore, is always a 'traitor'. And each one of you must become, a 'traitor', too, so that the divine spirits can capture the fortress and transform the whole earth.

So, make up your minds ; it is time to form a brotherhood of very advanced beings devoted to doing whatever they possibly can to open the gates and bring in the Heavenly Hosts so that they may transform the earth. And, as I have already told you, more and more workers will come and join in this work.

8

BROTHERHOOD,
A HIGHER STATE OF CONSCIOUSNESS

I

When we glance about us at the world, human society and the family, we see that everything is organized with a view to satisfying human nature, and this, in reality, means our animal nature, and all our most primitive instincts. All the rules and norms of society, all our criteria, even the education we give our children, are all designed to serve the prevailing mentality : to grab the biggest share for oneself, to take advantage of others, to become rich, to gain the upper hand. This is why we see so much rivalry and so many conflicts and massacres today.

And yet, when man was first made in the Lord's workshops, Cosmic Intelligence planted in him seeds that were destined to grow and blossom into qualities and virtues and sublime acts of abnegation and renunciation. From time to time, it is true, one does see these qualities in a few people. And the way they live and act leaves us in no doubt that a divine nature is manifesting itself through them.

But beings like this are so few and far between that they cannot influence the masses ; in fact they often fall a prey to the masses who are incapable of appreciating them, and they are persecuted and massacred.

In my talks to you I have often spoken about this all-important question of man's twofold nature : his lower, animal nature, which I call the personality, and that higher, divine nature, which is still dormant in each one of us because we have never taken the trouble to awaken it, and which I call the individuality. These two natures are so closely intertwined that it is not always possible to distinguish which one is manifesting itself at a given moment. Very often, in fact, someone will do something in the sincere conviction that he is acting with integrity and honesty, when, in fact, he is following his animal instincts : it is his lower nature that is manifesting itself. And if anarchy and egoism have become the order of the day, it is because most human beings think it is absolutely normal to obey their lower, animal nature, which demands that they satisfy all its whims at the expense of others, as though it were alone in the world.

And now, picture to yourself an Initiate, a Master, who wants to help human beings to free themselves from this morass, so he creates a Brotherhood in which they can learn to live in an atmosphere of peace and freedom. Nobody in that

Brotherhood has been hypnotized or bewitched ; on the contrary, everybody is free, lucid and independent, but in a spirit of collective harmony. And then, one day, someone who knows nothing of these new conceptions arrives and, naturally, all this is not to his liking. He is in violent reaction and spends his time criticizing everything : why does everyone here behave with such respect ? What is all that silence for ? You have all been hypnotized ; you're nothing but slaves ; you're all under a spell ; you must break free ! In other words : 'You must revert to chaos' ! With this kind of mentality, human beings are heading straight for disaster !

So many people are convinced that to be an anarchist and a rebel is to show oneself to be more intelligent, freer and stronger than others, but how wrong they are ! If they studied the human body, they would find that Cosmic Intelligence created it according to certain laws, and that these laws are also valid when transposed onto other planes. If the human organism is to be healthy and function correctly, all its cells must work together harmoniously and with disinterestedness, and not each one for itself : the stomach must not be content to digest for its own benefit, the heart to beat for itself or the lungs to breathe for themselves alone... nor the legs, nor the eyes, nor the ears nor the brain... All must work together for the whole. But with human beings today, it is 'each man for himself !' And this is why the body of humanity is sick, so sick that it is in danger of death.

The healthy functioning of an organism depends on all its parts respecting the law of sacrifice, of impersonality. When there is any manifestation of self-centredness, when some recalcitrant cells want to form a state within the State, the organism becomes ill. The rebellious cells form a tumour, a cancer that ravages the organism, because they refuse to obey the law of love and want to live exclusively for themselves.

Cosmic Intelligence speaks and explains things to us through our human nature. But we prefer to go and learn from diseased and decaying human beings, as though it were they who possessed the truth ! Nobody goes to the library of life to consult the book in which Nature has written it all down : a human being created by God.

The advantage of collective life is that it obliges the individual human being to tune in to others, and each one advances thanks to the fact that he is synchronized with the whole. And as the human collectivity tends towards harmony with a vaster collectivity, the cosmic collectivity, when a human being tries to live in harmony with others of his kind, he enters into contact with Cosmic Intelligence and receives its blessings.

Humanity is like one great orchestra. Each individual represents an instrument — clarinet, cello, trumpet, violin, piano, guitar, and so on. And the divine life which flows in every living creature, breathes into these instruments or touches their strings. Each individual creature produces a specific note and Cosmic Intelligence has tuned and harmonized all these notes so that they may form the one great symphony of the universe. It is only here, on earth, that this symphony does not exist, because human beings are guided by their instincts and passions and fail to vibrate as they were created to vibrate, to the rhythm of universal harmony. They cannot do so because their lower nature still restricts their field of consciousness. But once they have decided to work for the welfare of the collectivity, or rather, of the brotherhood, they will begin to vibrate on the same wavelength as the universe. And this accord will open the floodgates of Heaven, and celestial energies will flow freely through the world and sustain mankind with all the most beneficial currents from the cosmos. There is nothing worse than a purely personal life which is out of tune with the collective life of the universe, for it blocks up the channels through which cosmic energies should flow.

We must get back to the original harmony created by God. God created human beings so that they could all be in tune with each other like an orchestra. But no one has ever understood what an orchestra or a choir is. Our physical body, when it is in perfect condition, is a choir : all the cells sing together to produce well-being, joy and health. When our cells no longer sing in harmony, we feel ill, unbalanced and miserable, and illness takes different forms according to the different kinds of disharmony produced by our organs.

It has never occurred to anyone to interpret the fact that the members of an orchestra are not free to play whatever they please ; they have to respect the notes, the tempo and the shades of feeling indicated in the score, and if they refuse they are fired. Well, believe me : humanity is not a very good orchestra ; it produces too many discordant notes ! All the members sing at the tops of their voices and play whatever comes into their heads ; it is enough to make anyone stop up their ears. Every human being thinks he has the right to sing whatever he likes. It is only in Initiatic schools that they learn that they must harmonize with others. Before someone can harmonize with others, he needs to know that harmony is preferable ; secondly, he must aspire to it with all his heart, and, finally, he must make the necessary efforts and sacrifices to achieve it. And then ? And then, there is nothing more to be said : harmony speaks for itself.

So hold fast to this idea : that you must do everything in your power to accept the Great Universal White Brotherhood, for it is this that is the start-ing point of your evolution ; there is no other way. If happiness and prosperity have not yet established their reign on earth it is because humanity is still divided. Everybody looks after his own interests ; they feel no obligation to work for the good of the world ; they remain confined to the narrow circle of their own personality. But in these conditions the Kingdom of God will never be established on earth. The name of the Universal White Brotherhood im-plies a different kind of work, with different methods and a different ideal : the ideal of work-ing for the Kingdom of God and the happiness of all mankind. Everything is contained in those three words ; Universal White Brotherhood. Apparent-ly some people don't like this name ; it upsets them. That's too bad for them ; they don't know of what they are depriving themselves.

Try to imagine that you are a member of an or-chestra : you play your own score and, at the same time, the harmony produced by all the other in-struments of the orchestra delights and enchants you. Your part is to play only the music written on the score in front of you, but you are also touched by the beauty and harmony that surrounds you. Or take the example of a choir of mixed voices : each one sings his own few notes and each one is uplifted and entranced by the poetry and marvellous har-mony pouring in on him from every side !

The only thing I am interested in is your good ; nothing else. If that were not true, I would have swindled you out of your money and left you to your own resources a long time ago. It has certainly not been for lack of opportunity that I have never done so : several very rich women, for some reason I cannot understand, have wanted to marry me and give me all their money. But I never accepted ; I was not interested. So I have never become rich ! No, but I have kept my freedom so as to be able to help you. That is all that matters to me : to see you shining ever more brightly, to see you becoming more transparent and luminous, strong, powerful and happy. Why ? For my own personal satisfaction, that is all ! I want to be able to say to myself, 'You see, you have succeeded.' And now, I leave you to analyze this and determine for yourselves whether it is my personality or my individuality that is speaking !

I told you, once, that there was no such thing as a disinterested act, that even God Himself has an interest where we are concerned. Absolute disinterestedness simply does not exist ; what does exist are various shades or degrees of spiritual interest. Even when you have only one goal in mind : to make human beings happy, luminous and free, you still have an interest : that of being like the sun, like the Lord Himself. But this kind of interest is so disinterested that it belongs to a different category, it becomes divine, but it is still an interest. And I have an interest, a greater interest than any other : that of leaving the indelible imprint of the divine world on you so that, later, when you are far from me, you will remember these things.

II

Sometimes, when you are not feeling at your best, because you are badly dressed or out of sorts, you try to hide from others. At other times, on the contrary, you feel on top of your form and want to let others see you, to make yourself agreeable to them and receive something, if only approval, from them in return. All that is absolutely natural ! Even animals and birds have this instinct. They know what it is to be handsome or ugly. Look at the peacock : if he has lost his tail feathers he hides himself away, but when they are all there, he struts about and shows them off. But this rule does not apply only to external things. In fact, I dared to say, one day, that if someone did not want to live in a brotherhood, it was because he felt ugly inside himself. Yes, this is absolutely true. When you are full of good feelings and an overabundance of love, you ask nothing better than to pour it all out on others. There's too much of it ; you cannot keep it all to yourself ! And when you feel tired, out of sorts or disappointed, you feel the need to avoid others.

To want to live in a fraternal community, therefore, is a good sign, whereas it is a very bad sign to want to remain alone in one's own little corner. Perhaps, if that is your attitude, you imagine yourself to be very intelligent, but you are mistaken : your intelligence is flawed. For, I repeat, when one is truly rich inwardly, one feels the need to share one's wealth with others.

So, all those who want to live together in a fraternal community are welcome. Even if they have no very special qualifications, as long as they emanate brotherly love they are useful, for this is the element we need most. Intellectual and artistic gifts are not sufficient to improve the world ; in fact, there is already too much of that : there are too many intellectuals, too many scientists and artists, and not enough who love a fraternal way of life. When human beings begin to understand that it is the Brotherhood that will save the world, everything will change ; but that has not yet happened.

To be sure, the history of mankind shows that men realized a very long time ago that it was to their advantage to organize life in social groups ; otherwise they would still be spending their days hunting for food in the forests. The day they saw that it was better to unite in order to have many hands and many strong backs to share the load, everyone began to benefit from the new situation. While one was out fishing or hunting, another was weaving cloth, a third was building his hut, and so on. And in this way, each was at the service of all, and all benefited from the work of each. It is in this way that man advances : each one practises his own limited activity and all the advantages of society are at his disposal : libraries, hospitals, public transport, the protection of a police force, and so on. All that would be impossible if he lived alone. In this way man has used his intelligence to bring the organization of the collectivity to such a pitch of perfection that he now possesses the means to stir up the whole world.

Unfortunately, though, it is our intelligence that is not yet perfect, because it has always been cultivated for selfish purposes. It may seem that human beings have solved the problems of the collectivity, but their solutions are more apparent than real. Outwardly they have formed nations and societies, but men are still inwardly isolated, aggressive and hostile to others. At heart they are still cave-men : inwardly, each one still crouches in his own little hole in the ground. Outwardly, we see nations and societies whose members support each other, who have their armed forces, social security, family allowances and so on. But men have still not understood the true significance of their material progress. They have still not realized what all these facilities, possibilities and benefits mean, or how they can be transposed onto the inner plane. There is still a great deal of work to be done before human beings reach the same degree of unity and social organization, but on the inner, spiritual level, by working all together for the same goal.

Although they may not always realize it, the different countries still tend to work for separation and isolation. They have various official relations, of course : Ministries of Foreign Affairs, the diplomatic service, organizations for international cooperation and so on, but each country is still determined to remain separate and distinct. Each one wants to be considered a power to be reckoned with, and expects to be treated with due respect by other powers. They are not inwardly united at all. So we must continue to promote this inner fraternity ; we must continue to work to bring men, peoples and nations together so that they may reach the sublime consciousness of unity and live rich lives of inner and outer prosperity and abundance.

The proof that this question is still only half resolved can be seen in the fact that, in spite of their fantastic material progress, human beings are still inwardly anxious and unhappy, still poor, still cold, still groping in emptiness and darkness. So mankind is going to have to move on, to another stage which is still ahead of us. In the Western world, outwardly at least, almost everyone has what he needs ; almost everyone has the food and clothing he needs. Even the very poor, the drunks and the homeless, are picked up and cared for ; yes, there are people who are destitute but, usually, even they are cared for. Conditions are far better than in the past. Outwardly, yes ; they are. But inwardly ? This is the work of the future, my dear brothers and sisters : to reach the point where mankind enjoys, inwardly, all the possibilities it now enjoys, outwardly.

What prevents all men from forming the Universal White Brotherhood, from becoming brothers ? What is standing in their way ? I have already told you : an illusion ! They imagine that they will be much happier if they remain alone and apart ; and the years go by and instead of becoming happier, they become more and more miserable.

There is nothing to prevent each person from continuing to live his own life. That is absolutely normal ; no one is going to ask you to let yourself be absorbed by the lives of others. You have your own life, your own physical body ; you are a separate, independent being, but in the invisible world you must be united to all the other independent beings. The cells of our bodies do not all melt into one ; the cells of the heart are not identical with those of the stomach : each one has its own individuality. But the bonds of collaboration and affinity that unite them create that state of harmony

which we call health. Is that so difficult to understand ? Nobody is going to ask a black man to
become white, or a white man to become yellow.
No one is going to ask a Muhammadan to become
a Buddhist or a Buddhist to become a Christian.
The Christians have often sent missionaries to con-
vert Indians, African, and Asians, but in most cases
the result was none too good. Each one must retain his own particular characteristics, but there
must be a climate of understanding between them,
thanks to which they will be one in the divine world.

The ideal of the Universal White Brotherhood
is to teach human beings to work no longer exclusively for themselves, but for the whole world.
It is difficult, I know ; at the moment we are almost
alone in this work. But it is precisely when it is difficult that we must show the divine world that we
are faithful and true. When great numbers already
understand the necessity of this attitude we are trying to promote, we shall have less merit. It is now,
when conditions are so difficult, that it is merit-
orious to become a model. If, one day, Heaven
allows me to speak to the whole world, I shall say
this : 'Listen all of you ; you who are rich and and
you who are poor, you who are learned and you
who are ignorant : none of you knows where your
interest lies, and that is why you cannot break free
from all your difficulties. When it is a question of
exploiting others, of amusing yourselves or of mak-

ing war, you are all there, ready to join in. But when it is a question of creating conditions for the whole of mankind to live in happiness, you all disappear. So, this obviously means that you don't know where your best interests lie. You don't really want happiness ; if you did you would all work together to obtain it.'

Oh, yes. When it is a question of material goods, of money, property and houses, everybody is ready to pull together and devote all their energies to acquiring them. But when it is a question of men's happiness, of freedom and personal fulfilment for the whole world, they lose interest. How can you explain this ? When human beings understand the one simple question of their own best interest, all their problems will be solved.

In fact, this is the simplest, clearest thing in the world ; it is just that people have never stopped to think about it. They need someone to tell them, 'If you experience so much unhappiness and have so many difficulties in life, it is because that is what you want ; consciously or unconsciously that is what you are looking for. If you really wanted the opposite you could have it, today !' I tell you : human beings don't know where their interest lies. But I do ; I know that it lies in the Universal White Brotherhood, because it is here that they can learn to break out of their strait-jacket and bring all their desires, thoughts, interests and activity to bear on the collectivity, the universal dimension of life.

And now I must say just one more thing : all the spiritual movements that exist on earth are magnificent. They are all necessary : they all seek knowledge, power and realization. That is all well and good, but they still do not have that broader consciousness that would enable them to be less preoccupied, as in the past, with their own individual salvation, and give more time and effort to the collective aspect. It is good to want knowledge and power, but only as means to be used in reaching a much higher goal : the goal of brotherhood, of universal life.

History holds many examples of people who were endowed with amazing faculties, particularly of healing and clairvoyance, but they always used these gifts for their own enrichment or prestige ; they were not interested in using them for the establishment of the Kingdom of God and universal brotherhood. This is why, in spite of their extraordinary gifts and powers, they were never fully satisfied. Whereas those who work for the collectivity and the ideal of universality are happy ; even if they have neither exceptional faculties nor great powers, they are happy, because they are contributing to the strength of the egregor of the Universal White Brotherhood.

Every religious, political or cultural movement

and every country of the world forms an 'egregor'. An egregor is a psychic collective being formed by the thoughts, wishes and fluidic emanations of all the individual members of a collectivity working together towards the same goal. It often happens that the different egregors declare war on each other on the subtler planes of being ; in fact, clairvoyants sometimes see the battles of the egregors. Each one has its own particular colour and form. The egregor of France is a cock, that of Russia a bear, and so on. But neither the cock nor the bear, nor the tiger nor the dragon can solve the problems of the whole world. The whole of mankind together must now form the Egregor of the Dove of Peace. But who will do this if everyone works for himself ? The Christians ? Go and see whether Catholics and Protestants are working together for peace in Ireland !

The Universal White Brotherhood appeared on earth because the spirits on high decided it was time to introduce a new element, a new current amongst men. You will say that there are already a good many others : the Rosicrucians, the Theosophists and Anthroposophists, the Mazdaznans, the Knights of Malta, the Jehovah Witnesses, and even the Trumpets of the Lord... and surely that is enough ! No, it is not enough, for nothing very wonderful has come of all that so far. Each little clan works for its own interests, each one thinks that it alone possesses the truth, each one takes itself for the centre of the universe. In fact it would be true to say that it is the spiritual movements that are holding up the establishment of the Kingdom of God on earth ! Even if their goal is goodness and light, they are not working for the collectivity.

Only the Universal White Brotherhood accepts every single person in the whole world, with his own particular characteristics. It does not claim to know more than the other movements, or to be more gifted, more powerful or, still less, richer than they. They have all that, they are truly admirable and I have no intention of denigrating their value, I am not narrow-minded ; but they lack the new element that we have, the element of warmth, love and brotherly exchange. I have attended the meetings of many spiritual movements, and there was always such coldness, such pride and haughtiness. The Kingdom of God will never be established on earth with that kind of attitude. We, in the Brotherhood, have perhaps only one element, but it is the most important of all : the spirit of brotherliness. All the others are brimful with knowledge, wealth and psychic powers, but if the world is to become one great Family, it is the spirit of brotherliness that is needed, and not many people are trying to acquire that. But if, from now on, human beings decide to work for the benefit of the collective life, and not only for their own power, prestige, glory or enrichment, the Kingdom of God will come. It is so clear and straightforward : it is simply a question of working in a different direction.

The true meaning of life lies in collaborating in the work of the Spirits who guide us and who are with us to help us, and in convincing yourself that you want to change, that you want to work for a divine idea. If each one does this, the idea will grow and spread and sweep over the whole world, bringing all kinds of blessings and bringing to birth geniuses, saints and prophets. Nothing is more important than this work. If we don't participate in it, we are nothing more than walking corpses.

One day, you, too, will begin to see that human beings do not know where their best interest lies. At the moment they think they have found it in things that, in reality, can only weaken and enslave them. So they need a new light, and that new light can only come from beings who have studied and suffered in their quest for these truths. Obviously, nothing can be achieved in one day ; it all takes time and effort, but the time and effort are not important. The only thing that matters is to know that our interest lies in striving with all one's being towards a heavenly goal. If we have to suffer on the way, that does not matter. What does matter is to keep advancing towards the highest and best.

III

At first sight, when one looks at man as he now is, the notion that, one day, the whole world will be united in one great Family seems totally unrealistic. Outwardly, it is true, men are all so different from each other : colour, physical types, customs, culture and religions, are all different. If you tried to make Parisians and Eskimos live together, with Eskimos in Paris and Parisians in Lapland, it might be extremely complicated. But, in fact, if you examine the question more closely, you will understand that in their inner being all humans are alike ; on a higher level, in their higher Self, they all have the same needs, the same desires and the same ideal. But, of course, as they do not live their everyday lives in these higher regions, they cannot see themselves and each other on that level, and they do not know that they are all the same, all brothers and sisters. When they look at each other on the lower levels, they feel so different, so foreign and even opposed to each other, that they begin to hate each other and are ready to fight and kill.

Gradually, as human beings evolve, they will get to know each other better, and then they will see that they are all alike ; that all men aspire to joy and happiness, freedom, knowledge and light, and that all suffer in the same way. When they understand this, they will begin to realize that their differences are only external and that, under their different masks, all men are the same ; they are like actors who fight and kill each other on-stage, but off-stage they are all friends and members of the same troupe.

Human beings are all on a stage, acting out their roles in comedies or tragedies, whereas in real life they are all brothers and sisters. If the populations that go to war with each other realized that they were all citizens of the same fatherland on high, they would stop slaughtering each other. But this awareness has not yet manifested itself : human beings still live on too low a level, the level of their appetites and lusts, of their self-interest. In the long run they are going to have to become aware that they are all sons and daughters of the same Father and Mother, the Heavenly Father and the Supreme Mother ; and when they attain this level of consciousness their behaviour will change.

You must reflect about all this and study the question until you are fully convinced of this truth :

that the better one knows man in his higher dimension, the more obvious it becomes that all human beings are built on the same pattern and all have the same needs. Yes, there is still a great deal of work to be done inwardly, in order to awaken in oneself this sense of unity.

When human beings finally reach the point of admitting that their souls and spirits are one on high, they will form one great family, the great family of the Universal White Brotherhood, and wars will cease of themselves. Or rather, it would be more accurate to say that war will one day be waged with love : like the stars, human beings will shoot rays of love at each other. Yes, because, as I have already explained, the need to fight will never disappear, but the way in which this need manifests itself will change. The more highly evolved human beings become, the more the exchanges between them resemble those between the constellations and suns of the universe : exchanges of light and love.

When I was very young, in Bulgaria, I often slept out in the open, above the Rila lakes. It was at an altitude of 2,500 metres, and sometimes it would snow during the night and I would wake up to find myself half buried in snow. Ah, what wonderful memories I have of those days ! Very often, I would drop off to sleep while contemplating the stars, and this is how I first discovered that the stars had declared war amongst themselves, and that they fired light at each other : one day, human beings will wage war like that, with rays of love. Cosmic Intelligence will never destroy man's need to make war ; only the form that war takes will change. In the future, wars will not be fought with guns and bombs, but with light, colours and love. And what a war it will be ! I am all in favour of that kind of war ! In fact, I have already declared war, myself, on the whole of mankind. Ah, there is nothing more marvellous than this war !

So, there are elements and tendencies in man that no one will ever be able to change, but they can be steered in another direction : they can all be brought to converge on a single point, on the summit. Look at the pyramids. The shape of the pyramids is symbolic ; it indicates that everything must be made to converge towards a single point, the highest point : the First Cause, God. As long as all the different elements are scattered and divergent there will never be lasting peace.

As the saying has it : 'Know thyself'. We must know man in his external reality but also in his internal reality. And it is precisely on that level, on the inner, spiritual level, that all men are the same : whatever their race or degree of education, they have all been created and formed on the same pattern in the Lord's workshops. For the time being, they are so deeply embedded in matter, that they are bound to detest each other ; they are incapable of doing otherwise. Go and look at the way swamp creatures and the animals in the jungle behave : they spend their time attacking and devouring each other. And then go up much higher, and see how the angelic hierarchies behave, and you will see that they are constantly embracing and giving each other gifts. Yes, up above it is like that, but down below strife and hatred are the rule. This is why human beings, who have sunk so low, can do nothing but exterminate each other. And then people draw their so-called lesson from life, and say that man is a ravening wolf for his fellow man, and that the law of the jungle reigns on earth ! Yes, that is true if you remain on the lowest level. But the higher you go, the more love you will find. Go all the way to the sun and you will find nothing but love, and still more love ! If human beings could only rise high enough, they would be so dazzled and awed by that higher reality that they would immediately open their arms to each other, and the Golden Age would be upon us !

So I am obliged to say it again : without the light of the Teaching brought by the Universal White Brotherhood, we shall never achieve any progress. But with that light, everything is possible. Some have already understood and are working in this direction, but as those in power have not yet been influenced, they continue to do as they please, and the world is still in a state of misery and unrest. But if we continue our work, and continue to be truly united, one day we shall manage to shake the power of those who govern with cruelty and injustice, and they will be obliged either to change or to let others take their place. We are going to have to force them. Not by force of arms or threats, of course ; with nothing but the power of light, but we shall have to force them. If we can only be numerous enough, they will be obliged to pay attention to us. In the face of such light, love and harmony they will have no recourse but to capitulate.

We have every right to triumph over others, but only by the power of light and love. Nobody ever gained anything yet by rebellions and massacres. On the contrary, they only make things worse. I am a revolutionary, more revolutionary, in fact, than anyone ; but my way of being a revolutionary is different. History shows that after every revolution, things have very quickly gone back to what they were before : the same disorders, the same dishonesty, the same waste and injustice. So where is the improvement ? The oppressors and the oppressed have changed places, but they are still there ! No real improvement will ever be achieved by external changes, it is the mentality of human beings that has to change ; true revolution must take place in the minds of men.

Of course, I know that a lot of people are working for the good of mankind, for world peace ; but as they don't know what to base their work on, it is largely a wasted effort. True progress, true change takes place in the mind and heart and soul ; and it takes place thanks to the action of light. We shall never really be able to change anything for the better if we cling to the same egotistical, dishonest, treacherous mentality. How can any change be effective and worthwhile if the mentality remains what it is today ? We must aim at changing mentalities, because then society will automatically change, too. Everything depends on mentalities. And they can only be changed by a new, true and truly effective philosophy.

Everybody spends their time repeating that the world is going to the dogs, that things have got to change, but nobody offers any real solutions. Too many words are being spoken, too many books are being written, and love, the only cement capable of binding human beings together, is missing. It is true that, in every part of the world, we can see young people filled with enthusiasm and eager to do something, and they join together and form associations of various kinds. This is wonderful ! But as they have never been properly instructed, they do not know what to do or where to begin. They launch into ambitious undertakings without any idea of how complicated and difficult human nature is, and they soon find that they cannot agree, and then they start quarrelling and finally split up, forced to admit that they have done no better than their elders whom they were so ready to criticize. It is admirable to want to revolutionize the world, but to do it well you have to be properly versed in Initiatic Science, otherwise your attempts will be fruitless.

You must study human nature both in its baser manifestations and in its higher manifestations. As long as you know man only in his lowest nature, you are justified in saying that he is a wild beast. But you have to go beyond that and see that there is also a divinity hidden in man. The whole question is how to bring that hidden divinity out into the open ; this is where Initiatic Science is so necessary.

THE ANNUAL CONVENTIONS
AT THE BONFIN*

* The 'Bonfin' is the name of a property near Fréjus on the French Riviera. The members of the Universal White Brotherhood gather here in their hundreds every summer to study the Teaching of the Universal White Brotherhood, dispensed in the daily lectures of the Master Omraam Mikhaël Aïvanhov, and to put it into practice in all their activities as they work, pray, sing and eat together.

I

Just a few words, my dear brothers and sisters, with a view to making your time at the Bonfin easier for you. You have certainly already realized that your stay here is going to be rather strange, quite unlike anything you will experience anywhere else. This is why I want to explain a few things to you, otherwise you will just be bored and waste your time. Because here, you see, you will not find any of the fashionable amusements such as swimming pools, cinemas, casinos or games... How dull !

I travelled, once, on an ocean liner, and you know what that is like : the only thing that matters is to keep the passengers from being bored ! So, there are countless bars and swimming pools, dances, films and endless games and concerts. Since the opportunity offered, I was interested to see what life on board ship was like, but I was staggered to see all the different kinds of entertainment that were available all day and all night ! Life on a luxury liner is quite an accurate illustration of the mentality of most human beings, who are always looking for new ways of amusing themselves. As no one has ever revealed to them that they possess inner faculties and powers which, if awakened — and it is in their power to awaken them — would transform their existence and bring them peace, freedom and happiness, they are always looking for happiness from outside themselves ; the result is that they are always dissatisfied.

To be sure, none of us can get along without the help of certain external elements, but it is essential to emphasize and give priority to the possibilities of the inner world for, after all, man lives constantly in his own inner world. You are not always touching, tasting, listening to or looking at something external, whereas you are always with yourself, always in the world of your own thoughts and feelings, and yet you do not know how to use these things. As long as you rely on the world outside, you will always be disappointed. Every now and then you will feel that you have something to hold on to, and then, very shortly after, you will be left grasping emptiness : everything has faded away. Human beings are constantly seeking fulfilment, but they do not know that they must look for it within themselves.

And nor do you, my dear brothers and sisters. Nor do you know what is essential in life, and what your constant and most vital concern should be !

You still waste your time and energy on activities which you believe to be necessary to your happiness — but I very much doubt that they are ! Whatever you gain from them, it will not be what you are really looking for. For I know what man wants ; I know what human beings need, even if they themselves do not realize it. You will probably tell me that you know people who have absolutely no intellectual or artistic needs, and even less, any spiritual needs ; that they get along very well with purely physical pleasures. Yes, of course ; I know many people like that, myself. I have met a lot of people in a lot of different parts of the world, and I know that there are all sorts !

But what you don't realize is that those people, however crude and unfinished they may be today, come from the same workshops as the greatest geniuses, the greatest Initiates. It is not yet time for them to manifest the same gifts and virtues, but that time will come : one day, they, too, will seek immensity, plenitude, the Deity. One day, they, too, will understand that the objects and activities of the material plane are only necessary as a support, a vessel, an envelope to sustain, shelter or contain the divine life, the life of the spirit. And when they begin to understand that what they took for the real thing was only the wrapping, and that the essential core of things had been hidden from them, their way of looking at things will change. Yes, this is what counts : their way of looking at things. They will stop looking only at the containers and start taking an interest in the contents. Or perhaps, as they will have let the contents escape from the containers, they will start filling them up again and this will be the beginning of true life for them. You must never value the container more than the contents ; on the other hand you must not neglect or destroy it either, otherwise the contents will spill out and be lost.

I am telling you these things because the time has come for you to learn not to squander your energies : they are too precious. It was Heaven who gave them to you, and it is Heaven that is going to take stock of the use you make of them. If it sees that you devote the energies of your heart, mind and will to all kinds of inessentials, in one way or another it will take them away from you. I fully realize that many of you will not have much appetite for what I am saying : they would far rather be offered rather more succulent fare : delicious wines and hams, for instance, whether real or symbolic !

What are most people looking for when they go away for a holiday ? To work at improving themselves ? To purify and harmonize themselves and renew their contact with the Lord ? No, most people are looking forward to giving free rein to their lowest instincts and tendencies which they have been obliged to hold in check during the rest of the year. They could not do what they liked because, after all, they had to go to work every day and, besides, they were living amongst people who knew them ! But once they are away from home, amongst strangers, they can go overboard and indulge in whatever folly they like. Is it any wonder, in these conditions, that people, who should return from their holidays refreshed and rejuvenated, often get home limp and exhausted, and inextricably entangled in some new romantic involvement !

Disciples of the Universal White Brotherhood, on the contrary, learn to devote their holidays to purifying themselves and doing the spiritual work that they are not free to do during the rest of the year. This does not mean that we have no spiritual activities during the ten or eleven months of the working year : on the contrary. But the holidays enable us to devote all our time to this activity. The open air, the sea, the mountains, meeting other people and various recreational activities can all be excellent, but on condition that we have a lofty ideal that enables us to draw real benefit from them, instead of allowing ourselves to plunge into a whirl of animal passions.

So, let me warn any of you who may be here, at the Bonfin, for the first time, without really knowing what you have tumbled into : don't expect the kind of holidays you would have elsewhere. If

you do, you will soon be in a hurry to leave ! I have
seen this time and time again : for some people, ap-
parently, it is too difficult to remain in the light for
a few days in order to learn a few essential truths
that would illuminate and expand their consciousness. Human beings are not used to working
for any length of time on their inner landscape and,
in spite of the efforts of instructors who seek to
enlighten and liberate them and make their lives
easier, they remain bogged down in swampy
ground.

The day you begin to tire of so many futile activities, you will understand that, here, we are learning to seek the only thing that is essential : to vibrate
in harmony with all the forces of the cosmos so as
to become conductors of the Deity. Nothing else can
equal this. This I say and insist on ; and I shall continue to say and insist on it as long as I am with
you ; don't expect anything else of me ! In the
world, you are free to read the literature of every
country : enjoy it as much as you like when you are
at home, but you had better realize that when you
are here, you will never hear about anything but how
to improve and perfect yourselves, and you will
never be given the opportunity to do anything but
this. You will probably say, 'Oh, I'm fed up !' Yes,
you are fed up because you are not used to doing
this kind of work. But once you begin to feel that
divine forces are moving within you, our medita-

tions in the dining hall or on the Rock[1], at sunrise, will never last long enough for you, your hunger will never be completely satisfied.

Some of you will say, 'You're always talking about work, but we are tired. We've been working for the last ten or eleven months and now we need a rest.' Don't you know that the best kind of rest is to have a change of work ? And here, the work you are being offered is very different : it is not a question of going to an office or tinkering at some odd jobs in order to earn your living. It is a question of developing the divine nature that we have received from our Heavenly Father and which has been suffocated and buried during the year under all kinds of activities and preoccupations which were far from divine.

Many of you write and tell me how much they look forward to coming back to the Bonfin every year in order to enjoy the ideal conditions they find here, and which are so conducive to a more intense effort of purification. And when they first get here their faces bear the marks of the life they have had to lead in towns and cities, in the midst of noise and agitation, in an atmosphere polluted by smoke and,

1 The 'Rock' is a natural rocky plateau at the top of a hill near the Bonfin, to which the disciples go to meditate and watch the sunrise.

above all, by the anguish and disordered lives of
their friends and acquaintances. This is why each
one of you must resolve and constantly remember
to work with the truths received in this Initiatic
School, and never neglect any exercise that can help
you to maintain your efforts to improve. Otherwise
you will inevitably slip back into an ordinary way
of life and become more materialistic and even
selfish and evil, for this is what happens to those
whose lives are not inspired by a lofty ideal.

If you come here with the idea that you are going to go on living exactly as you have been living
in the world, it is not worth coming. You will only
be miserable, and become more and more tense and
worn out, and you will not get any of the benefits
you hoped for from your stay. But if you come here
in order to make the most of conditions that will
help you to restore order and harmony within
yourself, allow your divine nature to blossom and
undertake a gigantic work for the benefit of the
whole world, then, yes ! This is the place for you,
and you are very welcome !

So, for your own sake, for your own good and
your own peace of mind, I ask you to make the effort to use your stay here as well as you possibly
can, in harmony, love and light. Don't dwell on
what may be lacking, for in spite of all that is lacking — or perhaps because of all that is lacking —
you can grow and advance here better than

anywhere else. When material conditions are ideal, the will has less opportunity to manifest itself. It is in times of difficulty and privation that men find the incentive to make special efforts and transcend themselves. Anyone who has ever made his mark in the world has first had to surmount great difficulties and obstacles, often, even, to suffer persecution. The only conditions you should look for are those that allow you to exercise your will and communicate with the divine world. And you will find these conditions here, in the Brotherhood. You may not find the conditions you need for anything else, but for your spiritual elevation everything you need is there.

II

The Bonfin is like a clinic where you come for a cure of detoxification. All year long you have been living in conditions that were not particularly conducive to good health : your physical body and, especially, your etheric, astral and mental bodies are saturated with impurities that you want to get rid of in order to go back to the work that God is asking of you with renewed energy. Here you eat pure food, prepared and cooked by beings who are full of loving care ; you breathe pure air ; every morning you steep yourselves in the purity of the sun's rays, and now it is up to you to make an effort to introduce purity into your thoughts and feelings, your desires and plans. Take full advantage of the conditions you enjoy here, the beautiful weather and the peace and silence of the forest, to meditate and review your whole life and make up your minds, at last, to become true servants of God.

Since your reason for being here is to purify yourselves so as to be capable of carrying out a divine task, try to concentrate on that. Don't waste your energies on all kinds of other activities that can only introduce elements that distract you from your primary purpose. This is why I tell you that it is better not to go to the beach. It is very likely that, at the moment, you see nothing wrong with going to the beach. You say, 'But it does me good to go and walk along the beach and have a dip in the sea.' Yes, I know : the sea is a marvellous element, and God has given it tremendous powers ; but that is not sufficient reason to go and hang about on the beach like all those idle people who spend hours sprawling on the sand. What good can ever come of such idleness ? None ; on the contrary : it only makes you dull and limp.

You have an ideal, a goal in front of you, and at least for the few days you are here, you must devote yourselves entirely to that goal, and not try to keep one foot in the Bonfin and one foot somewhere else. If that is your attitude you will get no benefit from your stay. When you leave the Bonfin, you can go and bathe as much as you like ; but at least while you are here, consider that you are making a kind of retreat in order to find yourself and have some conversation with the divine world. Perhaps you think that I cannot see what goes on in your minds : just when you should be concentrating and meditating, many of you are distracted, your thoughts wander off to other things.

So it is far better to let yourselves be wholly absorbed and impregnated by something new ; if you feel that you simply must go and bathe, go ; but in that case, pick a spot away from other people. If you go and mix with all those people who have no spiritual ideal and who are only concerned with satisfying their appetites and desires, you will absorb all their fluidic emanations, and that is no way to purify and free yourself ! Of course, if you were really very strong and able to resist all those influences, if you were capable of transforming the impurities that you pick up, you could do whatever you please with impunity. But you are not strong : you are weak, you let yourselves be influenced ; and when you get back here, everything seems insipid and uninteresting. Whereas down at the beach there are crowds of people and lots of movement and noise — at least it's not boring ! So, as you are weak, you had better stay here. Otherwise, not only will you allow yourselves to be influenced, but when you come back you will influence others who are no stronger than you.

Try to understand what I am saying : I have nothing against your going for a swim, for water is a divine element. But if you do, choose a quiet spot where you can be in communion with the sun, with God and the Supreme Mother. Then, when you get back, you will bring a store of freshness and purity for all the other brothers and sisters. But if you mingle with the crowds on the beaches and then bring back that stale atmosphere, all those old vibrations that we are trying to get rid of, you will not be doing anyone any good !

Every day, I try to give you the best possible conditions for this work of regeneration, and all the help and advice you need, but you cannot see what use it can be to you. You still want to live the way you have always lived, and you feel hemmed in, here. Dear God, how difficult it is to change human nature ! You are always longing to plunge back into your old way of life, your old ideas, and then you wonder why you can't seem to solve any of your problems. Well, let me tell you why : it is precisely because you are always harking back to your old life, and your old life does not have the solutions you need. Write that down and remember it ! Don't expect anything, don't hope for anything from your old way of life. Is it so difficult to live a new life ? For my part, I find it the easiest and most agreeable thing in the world. I don't even have to make an effort ; it is the old way of life that is difficult for me !

So don't expect me to talk about anything but the new life : all that concerns the new life and how to live it. If that does not interest you, you had better go and look for what does interest you somewhere else, because with me you will always have to listen to the same subjects : the new life and how to breathe it, how to eat and drink and radiate it. This is the only thing that really matters ; this is what I am interested in. All the other branches of knowledge will open up to you once you have learned to live that new life. Yes, you will learn to recognize how the least little gesture or incident of your everyday life ties in to astrology or alchemy, the Cabbalah or magic. So, learn how to eat, breathe, behave, talk and think, and you will possess the foundations of these four fundamental sciences. You will even understand them in greater depth than those who study them intellectually.

You always think that I must be your source of knowledge. No, you must not hope for much from me : the new life that you live here will be your teacher. All I do is lead you to that new life, which is your true Master, a Master unequalled by any other.

I used to see so many brothers and sisters in Bulgaria, constantly hanging round the Master Peter Deunov's door, because they looked to him for everything : they expected him to heal and transform them, without their lifting a finger for themselves. And when he left for the next world it was they who were the most bitterly disappointed, because they had not advanced a single step ; they had learned nothing. They had spent years on the Master's doorstep thinking that, in that way they would get everything they needed from him... and they got nothing ! And yet, when the Master had seen what they were doing, he had warned them.

But it is a thankless task to try and instill some light into the heads of human beings when they are not ready to let go of their old ideas ! It is one thing to esteem and respect a Master ; it is quite another to expect him to do everything for you. It is you who must start working. If you do, all the treasures possessed by your Master will begin to seep into you, and even entities of the invisible world, when they see the efforts you are making, will come and help you. But first you have to work, because that is the only way to arouse your dormant capacities and get them to reveal themselves.

Our activities are based on the science of the harmonious and balanced development of man's many faculties. Yesterday I met a new brother who said, 'I realize that up to now I have always wanted to live an individualistic, selfish, useless life, and that that was not really living. But now I am determined to live a universal, divine life in the collectivity, in the Brotherhood.' 'That is wonderful !' I replied ; 'Now you can be sure of having the conditions you need in order to advance.'

And another brother told me, 'It's really fantastic, all that goes on here, and all that you reveal to us ! It's hard to imagine that somewhere like this actually exists on earth. But (for there is always a 'but') when I think that I'm going to have to go back and work with people who live such untidy, chaotic lives (I shall not tell you what his work is except that it is in the world of entertainment), I begin to wonder if there is any point in trying to transform my life. Since I'm obliged to go back and live the same kind of life as before, why try to change anything ?' I could only look at him, and say, 'What you are saying proves that you have still not understood the real usefulness and efficacy of our Teaching. For this is precisely what it does : it gives us the criteria and methods we need to face up to all the most difficult situations in life. Whereas, without the Teaching you would be swept away and drowned in an ocean of human passions and agitation. If you continue to reason along those lines you cannot expect to feel any desire to learn and transform yourself.' What I said astonished him ; it was quite new to him.

Life is difficult because we are constantly subjected to all kinds of temptations and pressures. But that does not mean that we have to give in : on the contrary ! It is infinitely preferable to study and keep practising so as to be strong and capable of overcoming and vanquishing every difficulty. To be sure, if you are to succeed you must have a philosophy, a high ideal, and also a Master. As long as you continue to live without a system, without an ideal and without a guide, you will be flung to and fro between conflicting forces, always at the mercy of circumstances. If you want to be safe, you must hang on to something higher so that the flood-tide of human passions cannot sweep you away. You are always complaining about feeling depressed and dispirited and without inspiration. Well, whose fault is that, if you insist on remaining on too low a level ? You have been given a ladder ; you have been shown a path and a safe refuge : why don't you climb on to a higher level ?

Yes, my dear brothers and sisters, you should thank Heaven all day long for the good conditions you have here. You have been rescued from a dusty, smoky, noisy world and brought here, where you can blossom and, at last, truly communicate with light. Why keep hankering for your old life ?

III

This morning, when I came up to the Rock for the sunrise, and greeted you all, I was astonished at what I saw : I have never seen you with such a glowing expression of fulfilment on your faces — all of you, without exception ! What happiness for me to see that ! No doubt it was the result of the little talk I gave you yesterday about the conscious exchange of light that you must learn to make when you meet and greet each other. But I was dumbfounded to see that you had put it into practice so promptly : your faces were alight and radiant ! How did you manage to produce such a transformation so quickly ?

Actually, there are all kinds of possibilities lying dormant in each one of you, and you never suspect how far-reaching they can be until you begin to feel their presence and to manifest them : then they reveal themselves for what they are. This morning you decided to be more conscious of what you were doing and to make your eyes and your greeting convey more life and greater love and light... and you succeeded ! Perhaps you will ask, 'But is that so important ?' Yes it is ; you have come here to learn exactly how important all these little gestures of your daily life are : every gesture you make and every word you say is important, but no one has ever taught you about that.

Look at the faces of all those you meet in the street or on trains or buses. How lifeless they look, or how tense or angry ! It is not a very pretty sight ! Often enough, even though you have absolutely no reason to feel sad or unhappy, you only have to go out into a crowded place to feel weighed down by all those negative vibrations. And then what do you do ? You arrive at the office or at home in the evening, feeling bad-tempered and depressed, and you pass on your mood to your family or your fellow-workers. This is how human beings continually poison the lives of those around them. Do you still believe that it is unimportant to show all those you meet an open, smiling friendly face ?

The question now, of course, is : once you have managed to create a beautiful frame of mind, how can you make it last ? First of all you must know an essential truth : each time you succeed in living a divine life, even if only for a second, all eternity is present in that second. You have made a print, a stereotype, and it will live for ever. This is true both of good and of evil.

When you experience a moment of harmony and plenitude the magic imprint of that experience is immediately created within you, and nothing can ever rub it out again. 'Well, if that's true,' you will say ; 'Why doesn't it last ? The very next minute, I feel just as anxious and discouraged as before. Why ?' Because life is a perpetual flowing ; moments follow each other in endless succession and you are not sufficiently vigilant to be able to stay with that magic imprint ; you allow yourself to be swept along by other ideas, other feelings and other activities. So other imprints come and take the place of that first one.

But it is important to know that the imprints of those magic moments are all filed away inside you, just like your own collection of records or tapes. And if, one day, you remember that you have a recording of a beautiful voice singing heavenly melodies, you can take it out and put it on your player, and there you are : captivated and entranced by the same beauty, reliving the same magic mood. You must think about this and remember to listen to these divine recordings over and over again.

Keep your recordings of all those precious moments in a safe place and try to relive them as often as possible. In fact, try to live only those moments ! You will say, 'Oh, that's impossible. I couldn't do it !' Yes, you could. Not at once, perhaps, but gradually ; when you are used to renewing and reliving these moments of harmonious, divine states of mind, you will understand that it is possible. To be sure, life can be very upsetting and fraught with problems, but believe me, it is still possible to renew and retain and cherish these moments of higher consciousness. If you cultivate the habit of vigilance that allows you to be permanently aware of the divine world, you will see that you will never be upset by anything for very long. Obviously, some things will still have the power to distress you briefly : some bad news, an illness or an accident, for instance. But if you are in the habit of treasuring these higher states of consciousness, you will rise above such problems much more quickly, because you will understand that God has given omnipotence to the spirit.

Unfortunately, human beings have never been educated in this way. They think that it is normal to fall from a good frame of mind back into their habitual state of disorder in which they suffer and cause suffering to others. Instead of trying to find a stable, immovable centre within themselves and making every effort to remain in that centre, their whole being lives in the flux and constant change of the external world. Like children, they are fascinated by what they see all round them. That is why they are so vulnerable and incapable of getting a grip on the situation. The whole of human education needs to be rethought in this sense. Those who have begun to understand, already feel that, whatever happens to them, they can stay on an even keel, whereas others are knocked completely off balance at the first sign of difficulty.

So treasure all the divine moments you experience, for as long as you possibly can, for each one of them is eternal and if you know how, you can get it back whenever you want to. It is etched into your being and no one can take it away from you. Go ahead, look for it : it is there !

If I am telling you all this today, it is because I was so struck, this morning, by all that you had managed to obtain. I thought to myself, 'If I don't say anything about it, I know what will happen : tomorrow that heavenly frame of mind will have disappeared without a trace. They will have gone back to what they were before, whereas they are capable of being always so full of joy, beauty and gladness and of communicating that gladness to all those they meet.'

So there you are : you must begin at the beginning. And what exactly is the beginning ? The beginning is to be wide awake, conscious, vigilant and attentive, to treasure each divine experience and never, never to think, 'Oh, it was all an illusion !' Human beings are really very bizarre ! They always think that whatever is beautiful is an illusion, whereas unhappiness, pain and disaster : that is real enough ! Well, for me it is just the opposite : the only reality is what is beautiful, good and divine. All the rest is illusion.

Why do people always have to talk about the sad, ugly things that happen ? Wherever they go they take their little pains and problems with them. Why ? Why do you always dwell on what is lacking instead of on what you have ? Our Brotherhood must be unique in this world. When others come here and see the light and love that streams from your faces, they will be astounded. There will be no need to explain anything ; they will only have to see you to exclaim, 'Ah, now I understand !' and at once, they, too, will begin to live the new life.

So, henceforth, try to work towards this. Tell a few lies, if need be : smile, even if you do not feel the least like smiling, and say that everything is wonderful ! That kind of lie is always permissible. It will certainly do more good than if you scowl at everybody to show what a bad mood you are in !

10

THE UNIVERSAL DIMENSION
OF ALL OUR ACTIVITIES

In the Brotherhood, we are in the habit of meditating together and also of singing, eating our meals and doing certain exercises together. Why ? Because the Universal White Brotherhood teaches new methods designed to help human beings to live a more fraternal way of life by developing a greater awareness of universality. The one thing that is most lacking amongst men, even amongst the members of spiritual movements, is the will to live a truly fraternal life together. In most of these movements it is the intellect that predominates. They are so proud of their knowledge and their psychic powers, and each one is separate and alone ; one does not sense any real love amongst them. Here, on the contrary, we try to cultivate real warmth and to be close to each other. When we sing together, for instance, we are contributing enormously to bringing our vibrations into unison, to attuning and harmonizing with each other.[1] The vibrations and auras of

1 See *Collection Izvor*, N° 223, chap. 6.

all the brothers and sisters blend and create the best possible conditions for luminous entities from the higher spheres to come and introduce their own vibrations into our midst. This is why the singing before meals is so important : it is an invitation to heavenly spirits to accompany and help us in these sacred instants in which, through the medium of the food we eat, we are in communion with the body and blood of Christ.

When we are all meditating and praying together, up on the Rock at sunrise, or here, in the dining hall, we are also creating unity amongst ourselves. Some of you may feel that you don't want unity ; you want to be different and apart from others. Well, you can do as you like, of course, but you must realize that in choosing to be apart, you are choosing the path that leads to death. The truth is that we are all built on the same model ; we all have the same needs : the need to understand, to love and to create. The pernicious philosophy according to which each one must be different and 'original', was invented by ignorant men and, in the last analysis, that much vaunted originality really is simply eccentricity and lack of balance ! No. Cosmic Intelligence has created all of us with a capacity for power, light, beauty and joy. And to attain this we must constantly draw closer to each other, not closer here, on the physical level, but on high, in the world of the soul and spirit from which we come. That is what we are doing when we meditate together.

These are the moments I love best : these moments of harmony and silence. Of course, I can meditate when I am alone, at home. But when we are all here together, in this climate of brotherhood, each one contributes something special, something different. You can compare it to those hostels in the mountains which supply only bunks to sleep on, but nothing to eat : each guest brings his own food. It is the same thing here ; not on the material plane, of course, but on the spiritual plane. Each one of you brings some fruit or vegetable from his garden, from his field, from his soul : a fluid, an emanation, a quality that we can all taste. Instead of being all alone and having nothing but your own radishes or tomatoes (symbolically speaking) to eat, because that is the only thing that grows in your garden, each one of you can eat a little of everything, because other kind brothers and sisters have brought something different : patience, gentleness, strength, health, love, tenderness, purity, intelligence, faith, hope and so on and so forth. There is enough, and to spare, for everybody !

This is the secret of the Brotherhood. If you remain alone, you will remain poor, whereas in the Brotherhood there is an abundance of everything and you can have a taste of it all. If you are feeling discouraged, for instance, you may not realize it, but the sight of all those happy, serene faces, will give you some tiny particles of their peace and gaiety and you will feel your courage surging back. If you remain alone you will never get rich ; in fact you will get poorer and poorer ; because when one is not getting richer one automatically gets poorer. Whereas in a collective, fraternal way of life, each one gains enormously, for men and women are the channels through which Heaven distributes its wealth. As soon as you understand this you will no longer be able to do without the Brotherhood.

For me it is as clear as crystal : even if I can pray and meditate alone, at home, I prefer to do so together with all of you. And how about you ? Do you feel the same way ? Yes, I can sense that you do, that you, too, have understood that your happiness is in this climate of brotherhood ; that this is where you can blossom and become freer. A great many people refuse to join a brotherhood because they are afraid of losing their originality and freedom. No, it is in the ordinary world that one loses one's freedom. Each individual behaves like everybody else ; each individual is quarrelsome and unhappy like everybody else ! Whereas here it is quite extraordinary ; the very fact that you accept the collective life gives you greater freedom and independence. More and more you begin to find yourself, to draw yourself up to your full stature and to discover that you are wonderfully well equipped for all kinds of magnificent undertakings for the benefit of the whole world.

To work alone and exclusively for one's own benefit : that is the old teaching, and it must now be replaced by something new. Of course, each one must have his own, individual work, but it must be for the good of the collectivity, because a collectivity must be formed of perfect individuals. And, as a matter of fact, when that point is reached, it is no longer simply a collectivity : it becomes a fraternity, a true brotherhood. A collectivity is not necessarily a brotherhood. It can be simply a group of people who all live and work at the same place : a school, a factory, a village or a town. But the individuals in that collectivity do not form a brotherhood, because they don't love each other ; they may not even know each other. Whereas a brotherhood is a collectivity animated by love, warmth and mutual support, in which each individual works consciously for the good of all. So we have to distinguish between three degrees : the individual life in which a person works alone and apart from others, isolated and turned in on himself ; the collective life in which individuals form groups because it is in their interest to do so, but without knowing or loving each other ; and finally the universal, fraternal life.

The Universal White Brotherhood brings a new philosophy which certainly does not reject the old ideal of individual perfection, but which gives individual perfection a new meaning, a new orientation, that of the perfection of the collectivity.

Take the example of our gymnastics.[2] When we do these exercises all together we form a tremendously powerful collective force. Each gesture, multiplied by hundreds of brothers and sisters, is a force, a wave which goes out from us and travels through space to touch the minds of men all over the world. The more numerous we are, and the more keenly aware we are, while doing these exercises, that we are creating currents of love and harmony, the more we can be sure that beneficial waves will sweep over the whole of mankind. It is important that you understand this.

You think that you are alone, separated from others. No ; that is an illusion. Even if you cannot see anything, whatever you do is reflected on the etheric, subtle plane. You are linked to each member of your family and of society, and the treasures and lights you receive when you advance, reflect on all those beings with whom you are connected. Thanks to your progress they, too, will progress. They may not know this, but Heaven knows it ; Heaven knows that it is thanks to you that they have made progress. And similarly, if you begin to lose your light

2 See *Complete Works*, vol. 13, Appendix, for a full description of these exercises.

and slide back, all those who are connected to you in any way, will feel the negative influence of what is happening to you. This is how we draw people after us, either to Heaven or to Hell, without being aware of it. Yes, we are responsible ; but human beings are totally ignorant of these laws, and it is this ignorance that is the cause of so much unhappiness. If you want to be useful and help the whole of mankind and even animals, plants and trees, you must rise to greater spiritual heights. In this way you draw the whole of creation upwards, and the invisible world will reward you for all the blessings that rain down on all creatures, thanks to you. But beware of the consequences to yourself if you lead them in the wrong direction !

There ! I have given you all kinds of extremely effective methods, and it is up to you, now, to learn to use them for your own fulfilment and that of the whole world. If your ideal is to live a truly sensible life, everything will be different. But as long as you have still not adopted that ideal, your inner forces and energies are not harnessed to anything that can give them direction, so everything is in chaos. Look at the lives of most human beings : what disorder, what confusion ! To be sure, some of them think they have an ideal, but more often than not it is the ideal of becoming rich and famous and influential. But that is not an ideal ! True, the lives of people like that are much more exciting than those of the limp and spineless people who are always tired ; they make excellent subjects for films or novels ! It is thrilling to read about all their adventures and exploits : how they betrayed a friend, how they got the better of all their rivals and how they enjoyed the fruits of their victory ! Yes, but Heaven will punish them for having used all their forces and gifts to satisfy their own egotistical lust for pleasure and power.

When you take part in our collective activities, here, you are participating in a tremendous work of magic. Think about this and set to work with ardour. A disciple of the Universal White Brotherhood must learn not to waste a minute ; he must learn to use every second of his time to do something salutary for himself and the whole world. It is thanks to the work we are doing here, that thousands of people are beginning to share our ideas of brotherhood and universality. Our ideas are spreading ; you must have noticed it ! Wherever you look : in the press, on radio and television and even in the speeches of a few politicians, you can find traces of our ideas. Not so long ago there was no sign of all this ; in fact, people scoffed at our ideas. But the Brotherhood continues to send out waves into the world and the brains which are capable of doing so tune in to them and pick them up. We are engaged in a gigantic work for the benefit of all mankind.

By the same author :
(translated from the French)

Izvor Collection

Self — 8. The Silent Voice of the Higher Self — 9. Only by Serving the Divine Nature — 10. Address the Higher Self in Others — 11. Man's Return to God, the Victory.

214 — HOPE FOR THE WORLD:
SPIRITUAL GALVANOPLASTY

1. What is Spiritual Galvanoplasty ? — 2. Reflections of the Two Principles — 3. Marriages Made in Heaven — 4. Love Freely Given — 5. Love on the Lower Plane — 6. Love on the Higher Plane — 7. Love's Goal is Light — 8. The Solar Nature of Sexual Energy — 9. Mankind Transformed — 10. The Original Experiment and the New One — 11. Replenish the Earth ! — 12. Woman's place — 13. The Cosmic Child.

215 — THE TRUE MEANING OF CHRIST'S TEACHING

1. 'Our Father Which Art in Heaven' — 2. 'My Father and I Are One' — 3. 'Be Ye Perfect, Even as Your Father Who is in Heaven is Perfect' — 4. 'Seek Ye First the Kingdom of God and His Justice' — 5. 'On Earth as it is in Heaven' — 6. 'He That Eateth My Flesh and Drinketh My Blood Hath Eternal Life' — 7. 'Father, Forgive Them, For They Know Not What They Do' — 8. 'Unto Him that Smiteth Thee on the One Cheek...' — 9. 'Watch and Pray'.

216 — THE LIVING BOOK OF NATURE

1. The Living Book of Nature — 2. Day and Night — 3. Spring Water or Stagnant Water — 4. Marriage, a Universal Symbol — 5. Distilling the Quintessence — 6. The Power of Fire — 7. The Naked Truth — 8. Building a House — 9. Red and White — 10. The River of Life — 11. The New Jerusalem — Perfect Man. I — The Gates. II — The Foundations — 12. Learning to Read and Write.

217 — NEW LIGHT ON THE GOSPELS

1. 'Men do not Put New Wine into Old Bottles' — 2. 'Except Ye Become as Little Children' — 3. The Unjust Stewart — 4. 'Lay up for Yourselves Treasures in Heaven' — 5. The Strait Gate — 6. 'Let Him Which is on the Housetop not Come

Down...' − 7. The Calming of the Storm − 8. The First Shall Be Last − 9. The Parable of the Five Wise and the Five Foolish Virgins − 10. 'This is Life Eternal, that they Might Know Thee the Only True God'.

218 − THE SYMBOLIC LANGUAGE OF GEOMETRICAL FIGURES

1. Geometrical Symbolism − 2. The Circle − 3. The Triangle − 4. The Pentagram − 5. The Pyramid − 6. The Cross − 7. The Quadrature of the Circle.

219 − MAN'S SUBTLE BODIES AND CENTRES
the Aura, the Solar Plexus, the Chakras...

1. Human Evolution and the Development of the Spiritual Organs − 2. The Aura − 3. The Solar Plexus − 4. The Hara Centre − 5. Kundalini Force − 6. The Chakras: The Chakra System I. − The Chakra System II. Ajna and Sahasrara.

220 − THE ZODIAC, KEY TO MAN AND TO THE UNIVERSE

1. The Enclosure of the Zodiac − 2. The Zodiac and the Forming of Man − 3. The Planetary Cycle of Hours and Days − 4. The Cross of Destiny − 5. The Axes of Aries-Libra and Taurus-Scorpio − 6. The Virgo-Pisces Axis − 7. The Leo-Aquarius Axis − 8. The Fire and Water Triangles − 9. The Philosophers' Stone : the Sun, the Moon and Mercury − 10. The Twelve Tribes of Israel and the Twelve Labours of Hercules in Relation to the Zodiac.

221 − TRUE ALCHEMY OR THE QUEST FOR PERFECTION

1. Spiritual Alchemy − 2. The Human Tree − 3. Character and Temperament − 4. Our Heritage from the Animal Kingdom − 5. Fear − 6. Stereotypes − 7. Grafting − 8. The Use of Energy − 9. Sacrifice, the Transmutation of Matter − 10. Vainglory and Divine Glory − 11. Pride and Humility − 12. The Sublimation of Sexual Energy.

222 — MAN'S PSYCHIC LIFE:
ELEMENTS AND STRUCTURES

1. Know Thyself — 2. The Synoptic Table — 3. Several Souls and Several Bodies — 4. Heart, Mind, Soul and Spirit — 5. The Apprenticeship of the Will — 6. Body, Soul and Spirit — 7. Outer Knowledge and Inner Knowledge — 8. From Intellect to Intelligence — 9. True Illumination — 10. The Causal Body — 11. Consciousness — 12. The Subconscious — 13. The Higher Self.

223 — CREATION: ARTISTIC AND SPIRITUAL

1. Art, Science and Religion — 2. The Divine Sources of Inspiration — 3. The Work of the Imagination — 4. Prose and Poetry — 5. The Human Voice — 6. Choral Singing — 7. How to Listen to Music — 8. The Magic Power of a Gesture — 9. Beauty — 10. Idealization as a Means of Creation — 11. A Living Masterpiece — 12. Building the Temple — Postface.

224 — THE POWERS OF THOUGHT

1. The Reality of Spiritual Work — 2. Thinking the Future — 3. Psychic Pollution — 4. Thoughts are Living Beings — 5. How Thought Produces Material Results — 6. Striking a Balance between Matter and Spirit — 7. The Strength of the Spirit — 8. Rules for Spiritual Work — 9. Thoughts as Weapons — 10. The Power of Concentration — 11. Meditation — 12. Creative Prayer — 13. Reaching for the Unattainable.

225 — HARMONY AND HEALTH

1. Life Comes First — 2. The World of Harmony — 3. Harmony and Health — 4. The Spiritual Foundations of Medicine — 5. Respiration and Nutrition — 6. Respiration: i. The Effects of Respiration on Health — ii. How to Melt into the Harmony of the Cosmos — 7. Nutrition on the Different Planes — 8. How to Become Tireless — 9. Cultivate an Attitude of Contentment.

226 — THE BOOK OF DIVINE MAGIC

1. The Danger of the Current Revival of Magic — 2. The Magic Circle of the Aura — 3. The Magic Wand — 4. The Magic

228 — LOOKING INTO THE INVISIBLE
Intuition, Clairvoyance, Dreams

By the same author
(translated from the French)

'Complete Works' Collection

Brochures :
New Presentation

Editor-Distributor

Editions PROSVETA S.A. – B.P. 12 – 83601 Fréjus Cedex (France)

Distributors

AUSTRIA
MANDALA
Verlagsauslieferung für Esoterik
A-6094 Axams, Innsbruckstraße 7

BELGIUM
PROSVETA BENELUX
Van Putlei 105 B-2548 Lint

N.V. MAKLU Somersstraat 13-15
B-2000 Antwerpen

VANDER S.A.
Av. des Volontaires 321
B-1150 Bruxelles

BRAZIL
NOBEL SA
Rua da Balsa, 559
CEP 02910 - São Paulo, SP

BRITISH ISLES
PROSVETA Ltd
The Doves Nest
Duddleswell Uckfield,
East Sussex TN 22 3JJ

Trade orders to :
ELEMENT Books Ltd
Unit 25 Longmead Shaftesbury
Dorset SP7 8PL

CANADA
PROSVETA Inc.
1565 Montée Masson
Duvernay est, Laval, Que. H7E 4P2

GERMANY
PROSVETA DEUTSCHLAND
Höhenbergweg 14
D - Bad Tölz

HOLLAND
STICHTING
PROSVETA NEDERLAND
Zeestraat 50
2042 LC Zandvoort

HONG KONG
HELIOS – J. Ryan
P.O. BOX 8503
General Post Office, Hong Kong

IRELAND
PROSVETA IRL.
84 Irishtown – Clonmel

ITALY
PROSVETA Coop. a r.l.
Cas. post. 13046 – 20130 Milano

LUXEMBOURG
PROSVETA BENELUX
Van Putlei 105 B-2548 Lint

NORWAY
PROSVETA NORDEN
Postboks 5101
1501 Moss

PORTUGAL
PUBLICAÇÕES
EUROPA-AMERICA Ltd
Est Lisboa-Sintra KM 14
2726 Mem Martins Codex

SPAIN
ASOCIACIÓN PROSVETA ESPAÑOLA
C/ Ausias March n° 23 Principal
SP-08010 Barcelona

SWITZERLAND
PROSVETA
Société Coopérative
CH - 1808 Les Monts-de-Corsier

UNITED STATES
PROSVETA U.S.A.
P.O. Box 49614
Los Angeles, California 90049

VENEZUELA
J.P. Leroy
Apartado 51 745
Sabana Grande
1050 A – Caracas

PRINTED IN FRANCE IN DECEMBER 1989
EDITIONS PROSVETA Z.I. DU CAPITOU,
B.P.12, 83601 FRÉJUS CEDEX
FRANCE

– N° d'impression : 1779 –
Dépôt légal : Décembre 1989
Printed in France